SOCIAL SCIENCES DIVISION
CHICAGO PUBLIC LIBRARY
400 SOUTH STATE STREET
CHICAGO, IL 60605

KABBALAH AND CRITICISM

D1118329

KABBALAH AND CRITICISM

Harold Bloom

continuum
LONDON • NEW YORK

2005

Continuum

15 East 26 Street
New York, NY 10010

The Tower Building
11 York Road
London SE1 7NX

www.continuumbooks.com

Copyright © 1975 by Harold Bloom

First published in 1975 by Seabury Press. First published by
Continuum in 1981.

All rights reserved. No part of this book may be reproduced, stored in
a retrieval system, or transmitted, in any form or by any means,
electronic, mechanical, photocopying, recording, or otherwise,
without the written permission of the publishers.

Typeset by Interactive Sciences, Gloucester, England

Printed in the United States of America

Library of Congress Cataloging-in-Publication Data

Bloom, Harold.
Kabbalah and criticism.
Originally published: New York: Seabury Press, 1975.
1. Cabala—History. 2. Criticism.   I. Title.
[BM526.B55   1982]   296.1'6   82–4674

ISBN 0-8264-1737-X

R0409098892

SOCIAL SCIENCES DIVISION
CHICAGO PUBLIC LIBRARY
400 SOUTH STATE STREET
CHICAGO, IL 60605

Contents

Prologue

That, too, I must have known

When the Holy One entered the Garden, a herald called out: "Disperse, O hosts, to the four corners of the world!"

1. One climbs to one side.
2. One climbs down on that side.
3. One enters between these two.
4. Two crown themselves with a third.
5. Three enter into one.
6. One comes forth in many colors.
7. Six come down on one side and six on the other.
8. Six enter into twelve.
9. Twelve agitate themselves to form twenty-two.
10. Six are contained in ten.
11. Ten are fixed in one.

Call this the text (*Zohar, Lech Lecha*, 77a) and quest after the interpretation. The hosts form a man, a tree, an alphabet, and every figure among the hosts is in every other figure, yet also acts upon every other figure. When the hosts gather together again, they form a chariot. All these things are known, and nothing is still to be gained by using the ancient names for all these, for they too are known. To seek after what is not known of this host, these ten primal numbers, and their fixation in one, as an eleventh, is to seek a primordial scheme after which the revisionary impulse seems to model itself. The first chapter of this book offers an account of that primordial scheme. In the second chapter, the scheme is related, in detail, to a theory of reading poetry. A manifesto for antithetical criticism, based on this theory, constitutes the third and final chapter.

*   *   *   *   *

. . . as much as to say, Mystically or enigmatically written; adding farther . . . they shall be only knowne to our hearers or disciples, and this closenesse Pythagoras *also having learned of those his Masters, and taught it his disciples, he was made the Master of Silence. And who, as all the doctrines hee delivered were (after the manner of the* Hebrewes, AEgyptians, *and most auncient Poets,) layd downe in enigmaticall and figurative notions, so one among other of his is this*—Give not readily thy right hand to every one, *by which Precept (sayes the profound* Iamblicus*) that great Master advertiseth that wee ought not to communicate to unworthy mindes, and not yet practized in the understanding of occulte doctrines, those misterious instructions that are only to bee opened (sayes he) and taught to sacred and sublime wits, and such as have been a long time exercised and versed in them.*

Now, from this meanes that the first auncients used, of delivering their knowledges thus among themselves by word of mouth; and by successive reception from them downe to after ages, That Art of mysticall writing by Numbers, wherein they couched under a fabulous attire, those their verball Instructions, was after, called Scientia Cabalae, *or the Science of reception:* Cabala *among the* Hebrewes *signifying no other than the Latine* receptio: *A learning by the auncients held in high estimation and reverence and not without great reason . . .*

HENRY REYNOLDS, *Mythomystes* (1632)

Kabbalah

"Kabbalah" has been, since about the year 1200, the popularly accepted word for Jewish esoteric teachings concerning God and everything God created. The word "Kabbalah" means "tradition," in the particular sense of "reception," and at first referred to the whole of Oral Law. But there existed among the Jews, both in their homeland and in Egypt, during the time of ferment when Christianity began, a considerable body of theosophical and mystical lore. These speculations and beliefs appear to have been influenced by Gnosticism and Neoplatonism, and it seems fair to characterize the history of subsequent Kabbalah as being a struggle between Gnostic and Neoplatonic tendencies, fought out on the quite alien ground of Judaism, which in its central development was to reject both modes of speculation. But Kabbalah went out and away from the main course of Jewish religious thought, and uncannily it has survived both Gnosticism and Neoplatonism, in that Kabbalah today retains a popular and apparently perpetual existence, while Gnosticism and Neoplatonism are the concern of only a few specialists. As I write, the desk in front of me has on it a series of paperback manuals, purchased in drugstores and at newsstands, with titles like *Tree of Life, Kabbalah: An Introduction, Kabbalah Today,* and *Understanding the Kabbalah*. There are no competing titles on Gnosticism today, nor on understanding Neoplatonism, and it is important that the continued popularity of Kabbalah be considered in any estimate of the phenomenon of the current survival and even revival of ancient esotericisms.

Popular handbooks of Kabbalah are not always very exact in their learning, and tend to be dangerously eager to mix Kabbalah up with nearly everything else in current religious enthusiasms, from Sufism to Hinduism. But this too by now is a Western tradition, for Christian popularizations of Kabbalah starting with the Renaissance compounded Kabbalah with a variety of non-Jewish notions, ranging from Tarot cards to the Trinity. A singular prestige has attended Kabbalah throughout its history, and such prestige again is worth contemporary consideration. Accompanying this prestige, which is the prestige of supposedly ultimate origins, is an extraordinary eclecticism, that contaminated Kabbalah with nearly every major occult or theosophical strain in the Renaissance and later in Enlightened Europe. A reader deeply versed in the interpenetrations of Kabbalah with these strains learns to be very tolerant of every popular version of Kabbalah he encounters. The five I have read recently were all terribly confused and confusing, but all were palpably sincere and even authentically enthusiastic in their obfuscations.

Yet educated readers need not rely upon such manuals. The lifework of Professor Gershom Scholem of the Hebrew University, Jerusalem, was summed up by him, magnificently, in the various articles on Kabbalah in the *Encyclopaedia Judaica*, only a few years ago. These entries, revised by Scholem, are now available in one large volume of nearly five hundred pages, published under the title *Kabbalah* by Quadrangle/The New York Times Book Company. Most of what follows in this essay is based upon either this book or on Scholem's other major studies of Kabbalah, several of which are easily available in American paperback reprints. Where I will depart from Scholem cannot be on any factual matters in Kabbalistic scholarship, but will concern only some suggestions on the continued relevance of Kabbalah for contemporary modes of interpretation, and a few personal speculations on how Kabbalah itself might be interpreted from some contemporary perspectives.

Scholem's massive achievement can be judged as being unique in modern humanistic scholarship, for he has made himself indispensable to all rational students of his subject. I will suggest later in this essay that Kabbalah is essentially a *vision of belatedness*, and I would praise Scholem above all for having transformed his own belatedness, in regard to the necessary anteriority of his own ancient subject, into a surprising earliness. Kabbalah is an extraordinary body of rhetoric or figurative language, and indeed is a theory of rhetoric, and Scholem's formidable achievement is as much rhetorical or figurative as it is historical. In this deep sense, Scholem has written a truly Kabbalistic account of Kabbalah, and more than any other modern scholar, working on a comparable scale, he has been wholly adequate to his great subject. He has the same relation to the texts he has edited and written commentaries upon, that a later poet like John Milton had to the earlier poets he absorbed and, in some ways, transcended. Scholem is a Miltonic figure in modern scholarship, and deserves to be honored as such.

2

Any brief account of Kabbalah, such as the one I am attempting here, has to begin with descriptions, however brief, of Gnosticism and of Neoplatonism, for these opposed visions are the starting-points of the more comprehensive vision of Kabbalah. To most modern sensibilities, Gnosticism has a strong and even dangerous appeal, frequently under other names, but Neoplatonism scarcely moves anyone in our time. William James reacted to the Neoplatonic Absolute or God, the One and the Good, by saying that "the stagnant felicity of the absolute's own perfection moves me as little as I move it." No one is going to argue with James now, but a thousand years and more of European cultural tradition would not have agreed with him. Neoplatonism was essentially the philosophy of one man, the Hellenic Egyptian Plotinus (205–270 A.D.), whose seminars in Rome were subsequently written out as the *Enneads* ("sets of nine"). Seeing himself as the continuator of Plato, Plotinus sought vindication for the three mystic and transcendent realities that he called "hypostases": the One or the Good, Intelligence, the Soul. Beneath these hypostases was the world of nature, including human bodies. To bridge the abyss between the unified Good and a universe of division and evil, Plotinus elaborated an extraordinary trope or figure of speech, "emanation." The One's plenitude was so great that its love, light, glory brimmed over, and without the One itself in any way decreasing, its glory descended, first into the realm of Intelligence (the Platonic Ideas or Ideal Forms), next into a region of Soul (including each of our souls) and at last into the body and nature. On this bottom level, evil exists, but only by virtue of its distance from the Good, its division of an ultimate Oneness into so many separate selves, so many objects. The body and nature are not bad, in the vision of Plotinus, but merely have gone too far away from their beloved fatherland. By an intellectual discipline, Plotinus held, we can return to the One even in this life.

Plotinus had a strong dislike for the Gnostics, against whom he wrote an eloquent treatise, calling them "those who say that the Maker of the world and the world are evil." There is no great scholarly book of our time on Neoplatonism (for many of the same reasons that there are no drugstore manuals) but there is a superb work, *The Gnostic Religion*, by Hans Jonas, a worthy complement to Scholem's *Kabbalah*. Jonas usefully compares Gnosticism to Nihilism and Existentialism, citing many analogues between Valentinus, the greatest of the Gnostic speculators, and the philosopher Heidegger. Gnosticism, according to Jonas, is the extremist version of the syncretic, general religion that dominated the eastern Mediterranean world during the first two Christian centuries. Jonas refers to this general religion of that period as a "dualistic transcendent religion of salvation." "Dualistic" here means that reality is polarized into: God against the creation, spirit against matter, good against evil, soul against the body. "Transcendent" here means that God and salvation are alike trans-mundane, beyond our world. Gnosticism takes its name from *gnosis*, a Greek word for "knowledge." Though the Church Fathers attacked Gnosticism as a Christian heresy, it appears to have preceded Christianity, both among the Jews and the Hellenes. Gnostic "knowledge" is supposed knowledge "of God," and so is radically different from all other knowledge, for the *gnosis* is the only form that salvation can take, according to its believers. This is therefore not rational knowledge, for it involves God knowing the Gnostic adept, even as the Gnostic knows Him.

Gnosticism was always anti-Jewish, even when it rose among Jews or Jewish Christians, for its radical dualism of an alien God set against an evil universe is a total contradiction of the central Jewish tradition, in which a transcendent God allows Himself to be known by His people as an immediate Presence, when He chooses, and in which his Creation is good except as it has been marred or altered by man's disobedience or wickedness. Confronted by the Gnostic vision of a world evilly made by hostile demons, the Talmudic rabbis rejected this religion of the alien God with a moral passion surpassing the parallel denunciations made by Plotinus. We can contrast here the most famous formula of Valentinian *gnosis* with an equally famous rabbinic pronouncement of anathema upon such speculations:

> What makes us free is the knowledge who we were, what we have become; where we were, wherein we have been thrown; whereto we speed, wherefrom we are redeemed; what is birth and what is rebirth.

Whosoever speculated on these four things, it were better for him if he had not come into the world—what is above? what is beneath? what was beforetime? and what will be hereafter?

The rabbis believed such speculation to be morally unhealthy, a judgment amply vindicated by the sexual libertinism of many Gnostics. Since Kabbalah, in all of its earlier phases, remained a wholly orthodox Jewish phenomenon, in belief and in moral behavior, it seems a puzzle that Kabbalah had so large a Gnostic content. This puzzle can be clarified by even the briefest account of the origins of the Kabbalah. Kabbalah proper begins in twelfth-century Provence, but Scholem and others have traced its direct descent from the earliest Jewish esotericism, the apocalyptic writings of which the Book of Enoch is the most formidable. This earliest Jewish theosophy and mysticism centered about two Biblical texts, the first chapter of the prophet Ezekiel and the first chapter of Genesis. These gave impetus to two modes of visionary speculation, *ma'aseh merkabah* ("the work of the Chariot") and *ma'aseh bereshit* ("the work of creation"). These esoteric meditations were orthodox parallels to Gnostic reveries on the *pleroma*, the unfallen divine realm, and can be considered a kind of rabbinical quasi-Gnosticism, but this was not yet Kabbalah.

3

Some eight centuries after the Gnostics subsided, a short book, the *Sefer Yezirah* ("Book of Creation"), became widely circulated among learned Jews. There are at least half a dozen English translations of *Sefer Yezirah* available, and the little book probably will always be popular among esotericists. In itself, it is of no literary or spiritual value, but historically it is the true origin of Kabbalah. The date of its composition is wholly uncertain, but it may go back to the third century. Later Kabbalistic gossip attributed it to the great Rabbi Akiba, whom the Romans had martyred, which accounts for much of the book's prestige. What matters about *Sefer Yezirah* is that it introduced, in a very rudimentary form, the central structural notion of Kabbalah, the *Sefirot*, which in later works became the divine emanations by which all reality is structured. Since the next Kabbalistic text of importance, the *Sefer ha-Bahir*, was not written until the thirteenth century, and since that work presents the *Sefirot* in fuller but not final development, all students of Kabbalah necessarily confront the

problematic of a thousand years of oral tradition. All of Jewish mediev-
alism becomes a vast labyrinth in which the distinctive ideas of Kabbalah
were invented, revised and transmitted in an area ranging from Babylonia
to Poland. In these vast reaches of space and time, even Scholem becomes
baffled, for the very essence of oral tradition is that it should defeat all
historical and critical scholarship.

The "Book Bahir" (*bahir* means "bright") has been translated into
German by Scholem, another service, as this book is incoherent, and its
mixture of learned Hebrew and vernacular Aramaic makes it difficult even
for specialists. Though fragmentary, the *Bahir* is a book of some real literary
value, and truly begins the Kabbalistic style of parable and figurative
language. Its major figuration is certainly the *Sefirot*, the attributes of God
emanating out from an infinite center to every possible finite circum-
ference. Where the *Sefirot*, in the *Sefer Yezirah*, were only the ten primary
numbers, a neo-Pythagorean notion, in the *Bahir* they are divine principles
and powers, and supernal lights, aiding in the work of creation. But this
was still only a step towards the true emergence of Kabbalah, which took
place in thirteenth-century southern France, and then spread across the
border to find its home among the Jews of Spain, a process culminating in
the masterpiece or Bible of Kabbalah, the *Sefer ha-Zohar*. The *Zohar*
("splendor") was written by Moses de Leon between 1280 and 1286 in
Guadalajara, and with its circulation Kabbalah became a full-scale system
of speculation. After seven hundred years the *Zohar*, with all its faults,
remains the only indubitably great book in all of Western esotericism. Most
of the *Zohar* is written in Aramaic, but as an artificial, highly literary
language, rather than as a vernacular. There is an adequate five-volume
English translation (by Sperling and Simon) still in print, and well worth
reading, but it represents only a portion of the *Zohar*, which is however a
unique book in that it is impossible to say what a complete version of it
would be. The book (if it is a book) varies from manuscript to manuscript,
and seems more a collection of books or a small library than what
ordinarily we would describe as a self-contained work.

Rather than attempt a description of the *Zohar* here, I shall pass on
immediately to a summary account, largely following Scholem, of the basic
concepts and images of Kabbalah, and then return to glance at the *Zohar*
before giving a sketch of the later Kabbalah, which was created after the
Jews were exiled from Spain. For the *Zohar* is the central work of classical
Kabbalah, centering on the doctrine of the *Sefirot*, but Kabbalah from the
sixteenth century until today is a second or modern Kabbalah, largely the

creation of Isaac Luria of Safed in Palestine (1534–1572), and makes a rather different exposition.

Classical Kabbalah begins with a Neoplatonic vision of God. God is the *Ein-Sof* ("without end"), totally unknowable, and beyond representation, all images of whom are merely hyperboles. As *Ein-Sof* has no attributes, his first manifestation is necessarily as *ayin* ("nothing"). Genesis had said that God created the world out of nothing. Kabbalah took this over as a literal statement, but interpreted it revisionistically as meaning just the opposite of what it said. God, being "ayin," created the world out of "ayin," and thus created the world *out of himself*. The distinction between cause and effect was subverted by this initial Kabbalistic formula, and indeed such rhetorical subversion became a distinctive feature of Kabbalah: "cause" and "effect" are always reversible, for the Kabbalists regarded them as linguistic fictions, long before Nietzsche did.

Kabbalah, which thus from the start was revisionary in regard to Genesis (though asserting otherwise), was also revisionary of its pagan source in Neoplatonism. In Plotinus, emanation is a process *out from* God, but in Kabbalah the process must take place *within* God Himself. An even more crucial difference from Neoplatonism is that all Kabbalistic theories of emanation are also theories of language. As Scholem says, "the God who manifests Himself is the God who expresses Himself," which means that the *Sefirot* are primarily *language*, attributes of God that need to be described by the various names of God when he is at work in creation. The *Sefirot* are complex figurations for God, tropes or turns of language that *substitute* for God. Indeed, one can say that the *Sefirot* are like poems, in that they are names implying complex commentaries that make them into texts. They are not allegorical personifications, which is what all popular manuals of Kabbalah reduce them to, and though they have extraordinary potency, this is a power of signification rather than what we customarily think of as magic.

Sefirah, the singular form, would seem to suggest the Greek "sphere," but its actual source was the Hebrew *sappir* (for "sapphire"), and so the term referred primarily to God's radiance. Scholem gives a very suggestive list of Kabbalistic synonyms for the *Sefirot*: sayings, names, lights, powers, crowns, qualities, stages, garments, mirrors, shoots, sources, primal days, aspects, inner faces, and limbs of God. We can observe that rhetorically these range over the entire realm of the classical trope, including metaphor, metonymy, synecdoche, and hyperbole, even as the designation *ayin* for God was a simple irony (meaning one thing by saying another), and again even as the *merkabah* or chariot-throne was a metalepsis for God, that is, the transumptive trope-of-a-trope. At first the Kabbalists dared to identify the *Sefirot* with the actual substance of God, and the *Zohar* goes so far as to say of God and the *Sefirot*: "He is They, and They are He," which produces the rather dangerous formula that God and language are one and the same. But other Kabbalists warily regarded the *Sefirot* only as God's tools, vessels that are instruments for him, or as we might say, language is only God's tool or vessel. Moses Cordovero, the teacher of Luria and the greatest systemizer of Kabbalah, achieved the precarious balance of seeing the *Sefirot* as being at once somehow both God's vessels and His essence, but the conceptual difficulty remains right down to the present day, and has its exact analogues in certain current debates about the relationship between language and thought.

The *Sefirot* then are ten complex images for God in His process of creation, with an interplay between literal and figurative meaning going on within each *Sefirah*. There is a fairly fixed and definite and by now common ordering for the *Sefirot*:

1. *Keter Elyon* or *Keter* (the "supreme crown")
2. *Hokmah* ("wisdom")
3. *Binah* ("intelligence")
4. *Gedullah* ("greatness") or *Hesed* ("love")
5. *Gevurah* ("power") or *Din* ("judgment" or "rigor")
6. *Tiferet* ("beauty") or *Rahamin* ("mercy")
7. *Nezah* ("victory" or "lasting endurance")
8. *Hod* ("majesty")
9. *Yesod* ("foundation")
10. *Malkhut* ("kingdom")

It is best to consider these allegorical images as carefully as space allows, for the interplay of these images in some sense *is* the classical or Zoharic Kabbalah, though *not* the later Kabbalah of Luria, out of which finally the Hasidic movement was to emerge. It is not a negative criticism of Scholem to say that the *Sefirot* have not interested him greatly. Scarcely a dozen pages out of the five hundred in *Kabbalah* are devoted to the details of *Sefirot* symbolism, just as only ten pages of the four hundred and fifty of the earlier *Major Trends In Jewish Mysticism* by Scholem were concerned with expounding the *Sefirot*. Scholem is impatient with them, and prefers to examine larger mythological and historical aspects of Kabbalah. In contrast, popular expositions of Kabbalah for many centuries down to the drugstore present tend to talk about nothing but the *Sefirot*. What is their fascination for so many learned minds, as well as for the popular imagination? Contemporary readers encounter the *Sefirot* in curious places, such as Malcolm Lowry's *Under the Volcano* or Thomas Pynchon's *Gravity's Rainbow*, where these fundamental images of Kabbalah are used to suggest tragic patterns of over-determination, by which our lives are somehow lived for us in spite of ourselves. Like the Tarot cards and astrology, with which popular tradition has compounded them, the *Sefirot* fascinate because they suggest an immutable knowledge of a final reality that stands behind our world of appearances. In some sense the *Sefirot* have become the staple of a popular Platonism or Hegelianism, a kind of magic Idealism. Popular Kabbalism has understood, somehow, that the *Sefirot* are neither *things* nor *acts*, but rather are *relational events*, and so are persuasive representations of what ordinary people encounter as the inner reality of their lives.

Keter, the "crown," is the primal Will of the Creator, and is scarcely distinguishable from the *Ein-Sof*, except as being first effect to His first cause. But, though an effect, *Keter* is no part of the Creation, which reflects *Keter* but cannot absorb it. As it cannot be compared to any other image, it must be called *ayin*, a "nothingness," an object of quest that is also the subject of any search. As a Name of God, *Keter* is the *Ehyeh* of the great declaration of God to Moses in Exodus 3:14. God says *Ehyeh asher Ehyeh*, "I Am That I Am," but the Kabbalists refused to interpret this as mere "being." To them, *Keter* was at once *Ehyeh* and *ayin*, being and nothingness, a cause of all causes and no cause at all, beyond action. If Kabbalah can be interpreted, as I think it can, as a theory of influence, then *Keter* is the paradoxical idea of influence itself. The irony of all influence, initially, is that the source is emptied out into a state of absence, in order for the receiver to accommodate the influx of apparent being. This may be why we use the word "influence," originally an astral term referring to the occult effect of the stars upon men.

Below *Keter* as crown, the *Sefirot* were generally depicted as a "tree of emanation," as in the simple vision of influence. This tree grows downward, as any map of influence must. As frequent a depiction of the *Sefirot* is the "reversed tree," in which the emanations are arranged in the form of a man. In either image, the right hand side begins with the first attribute proper, *Hokmah*, generally translated as "wisdom," but better understood as something like God's meditation or contemplation of Himself, and frequently called the "father of fathers" or the uncreated Tables of the Law. Freud's imago of the father is a close enough contemporary translation.

The matching imago of the mother, on the left side, is *Binah*, usually rendered as "intelligence," but meaning something more like a passive understanding (Kabbalah is nothing if not sexist). *Binah* is sometimes imaged as a mirror (very much in a Gnostic tradition) in which God enjoys contemplating Himself. We can call *Keter* the Divine self-consciousness, *Hokmah* the active principle of knowing, and *Binah* the known, or reflection upon knowledge, or the veil through which God's "wisdom" shines. In another Kabbalistic image, certainly derived from Neoplatonism, *Binah* as mirror acts as a prism, breaking open Divine light into apprehensible colors.

The seven lesser *Sefirot* are the more immediate attributes of creation, moving out from *Binah* in its role of supreme mother. Where the three upper *Sefirot* together form *Arikh anpin* (Aramaic for "long face"), the great or transcendental "face" of God, the seven lower emanations form the "short face" or *Zeir anpin*, the immanent countenance of God, and sometimes are called the *Sefirot* of "construction." Unlike the Great Face, the constructive principles are conceived by analogy, and so are nearly identical with the principles of figurative or poetic language. The first, on the father's or right-hand side, most often called *Hesed*, is love in the particular sense of God's Covenant love, *caritas* or "grace" in Christian interpretation. Its matching component on the mother's or left-hand side is most often called *Din*, "severity" or "rigorous judgment." God's Covenant love requires a limit or outward boundary, which is provided by *Din*. This makes *Din* the Kabbalistic equivalent of the Orphic and Platonic *Ananke* or Necessity, the law of the cosmos. Creation, for the Kabbalah, depends upon the perpetual balance and oscillation of *Hesed* and *Din* as antithetical principles.

It is an unintentional irony of the *Sefirot* that they increase enormously in human and imaginative interest as they descend closer to our condition. Even the most exalted of Kabbalist writers relax and are more inventive when they reach the lower half of the Sefirotic tree. With the sixth *Sefirah*, *Tiferet*, the "mercy" or Heart of God, we are in the aesthetic realm of God's "beauty," which for the Kabbalah is all the beauty there is. *Tiferet* is the principle of mediation, reconciling the "above" and the "below" on the Tree, and also drawing together the right side and the left side, masculine and feminine. All Kabbalistic references to centering are always to *Tiferet*, and *Tiferet* sometimes stands by itself for the "small face" or God's immanence, and is frequently spoken of as the dwelling-place of the *Shekhinah* or "Divine Presence" (of which more later). In Kabbalistic dialectic, *Tiferet* completes the second triad of *Hesed-Din-Tiferet*, and governs the third triad of *Nezah-Hod-Yesod*.

Nezah or God's "victory" emanates from *Hesed*, and represents the power of nature to increase itself, in a kind of apotheosis of male force. *Hod*, the female counterpart emanating from *Din*, is a kind of equivalent to "mother nature" in the Western Romantic sense (a Kabbalist would have called Wordsworth's or Emerson's Nature by the name of *Hod*). *Hod* is "majesty" of the merely natural sort, but for the Kabbalah nothing of course is merely natural. Out of the creative strife of *Nezah* and *Hod* comes *Yesod*, "foundation," which is at once human male sexuality, and the ongoing balance of nature.

The tenth and last of the *Sefirot* is properly the most fascinating, *Malkhut* or "kingdom," where "kingdom" refers to God's immanence in nature. From *Tiferet*, *Malkhut* inherits the *Shekhinah*, and manifests that glory of God in His world. So *Malkhut* is called the "descent," meaning the descent of the *Shekhinah*. *Malkhut* is also called the "lower mother" as against the "higher mother" of *Binah*. As the closest of the *Sefirot* to us, *Malkhut* sums them up, and makes the world of emanation a pragmatic unity. The Kabbalist encounters the *Sefirot* only through *Malkhut*, which makes of Kabbalism necessarily a sexual mysticism or erotic theosophy.

4

In their total structure, the *Sefirot* are identified with the *Merkabah* or "celestial chariot" in which the prophet Ezekiel saw the Divine manifest itself. This identification led to a series of further symbolic analogies or correspondences—cosmological, philosophical, psychological, indeed every area in which over-determined meanings could be plotted out. Popular Kabbalism concerns itself with these overdeterminations, but they are not the prime spiritual significance of the *Sefirot*. That significance comes in the inter-relationships of the *Sefirot*, their reflections of one another within themselves.

The great master of these reflections was Moses Cordovero (1522–70), the best example of a systematic thinker ever to appear among Kabbalists. But the movement from the *Zohar* to Cordovero and on to Cordovero's pupil and surpasser, Luria, returns us from doctrine to history, for the later

Kabbalah is the product of a second and intensified Exile, following the expulsion of the Jews from Spain in 1492. Perhaps Scholem's greatest achievement as a scholar has been his analysis of Lurianic Kabbalah as a Myth of Exile. The *Sefirot*, though they lend themselves to such a myth, are too close to the unfallen worlds fully to accomodate fresh onsets of historical suffering. I touch here upon what I take to be the deepest meaning of Kabbalah, and will digress upon it, before returning to problems of theosophical meaning.

Louis Ginzberg, one of the greatest of modern Talmudists, introduced the Palestinian Talmud by remarking that post-Biblical Jewish literature was "predominantly interpretative and commentative." This is true even of Kabbalah, which is curious for a body of work professedly mystical and speculative, even indeed mythopoeic. But this emphasis upon *interpretation* is finally what distinguishes Kabbalah from nearly every other variety of mysticism or theosophy, East or West. The Kabbalists of medieval Spain, and their Palestinian successors after the expulsion from Spain, confronted a peculiar psychological problem, one that demanded a revisionist solution. How does one accommodate a fresh and vital new religious impulse, in a precarious and even catastrophic time of troubles, when one inherits a religious tradition already so rich and coherent that it allows very little room for fresh revelations or even speculations? The Kabbalists were in no position to formulate or even re-formulate much of anything in their religion. Given to them already was not only a massive and completed Scripture, but an even more massive and intellectually finished structure of every kind of commentary and interpretation. Their stance in relation to all this tradition became, I think, the classic paradigm upon which Western revisionism in all areas was to model itself ever since, usually in rather indirect emulation. For the Kabbalists developed implicitly a *psychology of belatedness*, and with it an explicit, rhetorical series of techniques for opening Scripture and even received commentary to their own historical sufferings, and to their own, new theosophical insights. Their achievement was not just to restore Gnosis and mythology to a Judaism which had purged itself of such elements, but more crucially to provide the masses of suffering Jewry with a more immediate and experiential personal faith than the strength of orthodox tradition might have allowed. Hasidism was the ultimate descendant of Kabbalah, and can be regarded as the more positive ultimate achievement of a movement that led, in its darker aspects, to morasses of magic and superstition, and to false Messiahs and even apostates.

The *Zohar*, astonishingly beautiful as it frequently is, is not in itself greatly representative of what became, from the Spanish Exile on, the true voice of Kabbalah. Though Cordovero and Luria derived fundamentally from the *Zohar*, their systems and visions actually have little in common with it. The *Zohar* is organized as an apparent commentary upon Scripture, just as much of the later Kabbalah is organized as an apparent commentary upon the *Zohar*, but it is the genius of revisionism to swerve so far from its canonical texts as to make the ancestral voices into even their own opposites. A contemporary reader encountering the *Zohar* will have trouble finding in it a clear statement about the structure and function of the *Sefirot*, let alone any of the more complex refinements of Kabbalah. Such a reader will find himself confronted by hundreds of homilies and little stories, many of them haunting in their enigmas, but finally compelling the reader to wish that the *Zohar* would obey its own injunction about how to interpret Scripture or the Torah:

As wine in a jar, if it is to keep, so is the Torah, contained within its outer garment. Such a garment is made up of many stories, but we, we are required to pierce the garment.

To pierce the garment of the *Zohar* is almost impossible, but in some sense that was the achievement of Cordovero and of Luria, to whose doctrines I now turn.

5

Scholem makes the point that after 1492 and the fresh dispersal of the Jews, the Kabbalah ceased to be as esoteric and became "public property." From about 1530 on, Safed in Palestine became the center of the new Kabbalah, and from Safed there emanated out to the Diaspora what became a new popular religion, which captured much of Judaism, and has left an influence (now much diminished) on it ever since. Isaac Luria was much the largest source of this new religion, and will receive more analysis here, as he does in Scholem, but Cordovero was a clearer and more systematic theorist, and some account of his ideas remains the best introduction to the intricacies of the Lurianic Kabbalah.

As early as the thirteenth century, Kabbalists spoke of the *Sefirot* reflecting themselves within themselves, so that each "contained" all the others. Complex systems of pathways of *Sefirot* within *Sefirot* were set up, and meditation upon these pathways became the characteristic Kabbalistic exercise, whether in vision, prayer or intellectual speculation. This theosophical path-breaking becomes in Cordovero what Ginzberg and other scholars have described accurately as a theory of influence. Cordovero invented a new category, *behinot*, to convey the multiform aspects within each *Sefirah*, aspects that account for the links between *Sefirot*. These are the six *behinot* or phases of the ten *Sefirot*, as differentiated by Cordovero: 1) Concealed before manifestation within the preceding *Sefirah*; 2) Actual manifestation in the preceding *Sefirah*; 3) Appearance as *Sefirah* in its own name; 4) Aspect that gives power to the *Sefirah* above it, so as to enable that *Sefirah* to be strong enough to emanate yet further *Sefirot*; 5) Aspect that gives power to the *Sefirah* itself to emanate out the other *Sefirot* still concealed within it; 6) Aspect by which the following *Sefirah* is in turn emanated out to its own place, after which the cycle of the six *behinot* begins again.

This cycle may seem baffling at first, but is a remarkable theory of influence, as causal yet reversed relationships. To be understood today it needs translation into other terms, and these can be psychoanalytic, rhetorical or imagistic, for the six *behinot* can be interpreted as psychological mechanisms of defense, rhetorical tropes, or areas of poetic imagery (as I will indicate later in this essay). Whereas the *Sefirot*, as attributes of God, are manifestly supernatural channels of influence (or rhetorically speaking divine poems, each a text in itself), the *behinot* work more like human agencies, whether psychic or linguistic. Scholem indicates that, in Cordovero, the *Sefirot* "actually become the structural elements of all beings," but they do this only by their aspects or *behinot*. One might indeed call Cordovero the first Structuralist, an unacknowledged ancestor of many contemporary French theorists of the "human sciences."

In order to see precisely the great dialectical leap that Isaac Luria took away from his teacher, Cordovero, it is necessary to expound the true, dark heart of Kabbalah: its vision of the problem of evil. Scholem rightly remarks that Jewish philosophy was not very interested in the problem of evil, and it seems just to observe that Talmudic tradition was also too healthy to brood excessively on evil. But Kabbalah departed both from normative Judaism and from Neoplatonism in its obsessive concern with evil. For Neoplatonism, evil has no metaphysical reality, but Gnosticism engaged evil as the reality of this world, which presumably is why Gnosticism now lives, under a variety of disguises, while Neoplatonism is the province of scholars. Probably, this is why the Lurianic Kabbalah came to dominate popular Judaism for many centuries, giving birth first to a series of false messiahs, and finally to the lasting glory of the Baal Shem Tov and his Hasidism.

The book *Bahir* speaks of the *Sefirah Gevurah* or *Din* as the Left Hand of God, and so as a permitted evil. Out of this came the Kabbalistic doctrine that located evil in what Freud called the superego, or in Kabbalistic terms the separation of *Din* from *Hesed*, stern judgment from love. The world of *Din* brought forth the *sitra ahra* or "the other side," the sinister qualities that came out of a Name of God, but then fell away from the Name.

The *Zohar* assigned to the *sitra ahra* ten *Sefirot* all its own, ten sinister crowns representing the remnants of worlds that God first made and then destroyed. In one of the great poetic images of esoteric tradition, Moses de Leon compared evil to the bark of the tree of the *Sefirot*, the *kelippah*. The creatures of this bark—Samael and his wife Lilith, or Satan and the chief of witches (of whom more later)—became in the *Zohar* almost worthy antagonists of God. *Kelippot*, conceived first as bark, became regarded also as husks or shells or broken vessels of evil. But even in the *Kelippot*, according to the *Zohar*, there abides a saving spark of good. This notion, that there are sparks in the *kelippot* that can be redeemed, and redeemed by the acts of men alone and not of God, became the starting point of Lurianic Kabbalah.

6

The problem of original genius in every intellectual area, past a certain date (a date upon which no two people can agree), is always located in the apparently opposed principles of continuity and discontinuity. Yet the very word Kabbalah means tradition, and every master of Kabbalah has stressed his own continuity rather than his discontinuity with previous speculators. Luria is extraordinarily original, indeed he may have been the only visionary in the entire history of Kabbalah whose basic ideas were original, since the entire tradition from the *Sefer Yezirah* through Cordovero is finally only an amalgam, however strangely shaped, of Neoplatonism and Gnosticism. But Luria had the originality of certain great poets—Dante, Milton, Blake—though since the important accounts of his visions are not written by him, but by rival and contrasting disciples, it is difficult to compare Luria's powers of invention to those of other creators.

Before Luria, all of Kabbalah saw creation as a progressive process, moving in one direction always, emanating out from God through the *Sefirot* to man, a movement in which each stage joined itself closely to the subsequent stage, without enormous leaps or backwards recoilings. In Luria, creation is a startlingly regressive process, one in which an abyss can separate any one stage from another, and in which catastrophe is always a central event. Reality for Luria is always a triple rhythm of contraction, breaking apart, and mending, a rhythm continuously present in time even as it first punctuated eternity.

Luria named this triple process: *zimzum, shevirah ha-kelim, tikkun* (contraction, the breaking-of-the-vessels, restitution). *Zimzum* originally seems to have meant a holding-in-of-the-breath, but Luria transformed the word into an idea of limitation, of God's hiding of Himself, or rather entering into Himself. In this contraction, God clears a space for creation, a not-God. This cleared point the *Zohar* had called *tehiru*, or fundamental space. Luria saw the *zimzum* as God's concentration within himself of the *Sefirah* of *Din*, rigor, but part of this power of stern judgment remained behind in the cleared *tehiru*, where it mixed together with the remnants of God's self-withdrawn light, called by Luria the *reshimu*. Into the mixture (out of which our world is to be formed), God sends a single letter, the *yod*, the first letter of his great name, YHWH, the Tetragrammaton. This *yod* is the active principle in creation, even as the *reshimu* is the passive principle.

This creation, according to Luria, was of *kelim*, "vessels," of which the culminating vessel was *Adam Kadmon* or primal Man. Two kinds of light had made these vessels, the new or incoming light that had accompanied the *yod* or Word of God, and the light left behind in the *tehiru* after the *zimzum*. The collision of lights is an enormously complex process, for which this present essay lacks space, but the crucial element in the complexity is that *Adam Kadmon*, man as he should be, is a kind of perpetual war of light-against-light. This war emanates out from his head in patterns of *writing*, which become fresh vessels-of-creation, newly manifested structures of *Sefirot*. But though the three upper *Sefirot* held firm, and contained the pugnacious light, the six *Sefirot* from *Hesed* to *Yesod* broke apart. This *shevirah*, breaking or scattering of the vessels, was caused by the force of the light hitting all-at-once, in what can be interpreted as too strong a force of *writing*, stronger than the "texts" of the lower *Sefirot* could sustain. Paradoxically God's Name was too strong for his Words, and the breaking of the vessels necessarily became a divine act of *substitution*, in which an original pattern yielded to a more chaotic one that nevertheless remained pattern, the guarantee of which was that the vessel of the tenth and last *Sefirah, Malkhut* or the female world, broke also but less severely than the other vessels splintered.

Though some of the light in the shattered vessels returned immediately to God, much of it fell down with the vessels, so as to form the *kelippot* or evil forces of the universe. But these *kelippot* still have pattern or design, as well as sparks-of-light imprisoned within them. Luria appears to have believed that all this catastrophe came about because of an original excess of *Din*, a plethora of rigor in God Himself, and it is in the *Sefirah* of *Din* that the smashing-apart begins. Scholem theorizes that Luria saw the whole function of creation as being God's catharsis of Himself, a vast sublimation in which His terrible rigor might find some peace. This is not unlike Freud's extraordinary explanation as to why people fall in love, which is to avoid an over-filled inner self. As man must love, in Freud's view, in order to avoid becoming sick, so Luria's God had to create, for His own health. But He could create only by catastrophe, in Luria's judgment, an opinion again very like that of Freud's disciple, Ferenczi, whose book *Thalassa* also ascribes every act of creation to a necessary catastrophe.

Remarkable as these first two stages of Luria's vision are, both *zimzum* and *shevirah* are less important in his doctrine than *tikkun*, the saving process of restoration and restitution, for this is the work of the human, taking place through a complex agency called the *parzufim* or "faces," the Lurianic equivalent of Cordovero's *behinot*. Scholem calls the *parzufim* "configurations" or *gestalten*, but like the *behinot* they seem to be at once psychic and linguistic, defense mechanisms and rhetorical tropes. As patterns of images, the *parzufim* organize the shattered world after the vessels have broken apart, and as principles of organization they substitute for or take the place of the *Sefirot*. *Keter* or the Crown is substituted for by the *parzuf* of *Arikh Anpin*, or God as the "long-faced one," that is to say, the God who is indulgent or forbearing even in fallen history. *Hokmah* and *Binah* are replaced by what Freud called the Imagos, *Abba* and *Imma*, "father" and "mother," who together create the fourth and most important *parzuf*, called *Ze'eir Anpin*, the "short-faced" or "impatient" or "unindulgent" God, who stands in judgment upon history. *Ze'eir Anpin* substitutes for the six lower *Sefirot*, from *Din* to *Yesod*, the six that broke apart most dreadfully. *Ze'eir Anpin* thus substitutes also quite directly for the *behinot* of Luria's teacher, Cordovero, and in some sense this *parzuf* can be considered as Luria's revisionist misprision or creative misunderstanding of his direct precursor's most original and important doctrine. Luria's last *parzuf* is called *Nukba de-Ze'eir*, the female of the impatient God, and substitutes for *Malkhut* or the Kingdom.

Together, the *parzufim* make up a new and second *Adam Kadmon*, for the *tikkun* or restoration of creation must be carried out by the religious acts of individual men, of all Jews struggling in the Exile, and indeed of all men and women struggling in the Exile that Luria saw as the universal human existence. The nature of such religious acts of *tikkun* is again too complex to define in my limited space, but essentially these are acts of meditation, acts that lift up and so liberate the fallen sparks of God from their imprisonment in the shards of the *kelippot*. Such acts of meditation are at once psychic and linguistic, but for Luria they are magical too, so that they enter the sphere of practical Kabbalah, a puzzling world that this essay must conclude by entering also, though again the entrance must be brief and tentative.

7

As a psychology of belatedness, Kabbalah manifests many prefigurations of Freudian doctrine. Yet most of these stem from the psychological notions of Neoplatonism, and are not original with Kabbalah. Thus, the Kabbalistic division of the soul into three parts is Neoplatonic, where the lowest soul is the *nefesh* or vital being with which everyone is born. The *ru'ah* or *anima* comes about later through a spiritual awakening, but only with the highest awakening is the true soul born, the *neshamah* or *spiritus*. Lurianic Kabbalah added further souls, so as to achieve a psychic cartography again too complex to sketch in so limited a space. But a more truly original notion, and one more prophetic of Freud, is the *zelem* or divine image in every man, first set forth in the *Zohar* and then developed by Luria and his disciples. The *zelem* is a modification of the later Neoplatonic idea of the Astral Body, a kind of quasi-material entity that holds together mind and physical body, and that survives the death of the body proper. In Lurianic Kabbalah, the Astral Body also serves the function of determining an individual human personality, so that the difference between one of us and another is not necessarily in any part of the soul, but in the enigmatic joining of soul and body, that is, in the relationship between our consciousness and our body. What makes us individual, our *zelem*, is the way our particular body feels about our psyche, or the way that psyche feels about the body to which it is linked. Scholem says that "without the *zelem* the soul would burn the body up with its fierce radiance," and one can add conversely that the body's desires would consume the soul without the *zelem*. It is as though Luria were saying, in our terms, that the body is the unconscious as far as the soul is concerned, or that the soul is the unconscious from the stance of the body.

It was only a step from the idea of the *zelem* to the Lurianic version of the transmigration of souls, called *gilgul*. Luria seems to have taught that there were families of souls, united by the root of a common spark. Each person can take up in himself the spark of another soul, of one of the dead, provided that he and the dead share the same root. This leads to the larger idea of a kind of Eternal Recurrence, with the saving difference that *gilgul* can be the final form of *tikkun*, in which the fallen soul can have its flaws repaired. The legend of the *dybbuk* is a negative version of the same idea.

With the idea of *gilgul*, speculative Kabbalah passes into practical Kabbalah, a world of "white" magic, dependent however entirely upon the sacredness of a divine language. It is very difficult to distinguish practical Kabbalah from the whole body of Jewish magic and superstition, the vast accumulation of folklore that so long a tradition brings forth. Very late or popular Kabbalah also became mixed with the "occult sciences," particularly astrology and alchemy, but these have little to do with Kabbalah proper.

Two areas of practical Kabbalah seem most authentic: demonology and what was called *Gematria*, the explanation of words according to their numerical values or the equivalents, by set rules. Kabbalistic demonology became absorbed by the wilder aspects of Hasidism, and is now familiar to a wide group of contemporary readers through the fiction of Singer. Such demonology ultimately centers upon two figures, Lilith and Samael. One can wonder why Lilith has not become the patroness of some of the more extreme manifestations of the Women's Liberation Movement, as her legendary career shows a strong counter-current of guilt towards women (and fear of them) moving in Kabbalah. Kabbalah enshrined the *Shekhinah* or Divine Presence in the shape of a woman, an image of splendor-in-exile, and the *Sefirot* are relatively fairly balanced between male and female sides. Yet Kabbalistic texts awaken into a peculiar vividness whenever Lilith is invoked. Though she seems to have begun as a Babylonian wind-demoness, she became very thoroughly naturalized in Judaic contexts. A pre-Kabbalistic legend held that she was Adam's first wife, and that she abandoned him on the issue of sexual equality, with the immediate cause of separation being that of positions in sexual intercourse, Adam favoring the missionary posture, while she insisted on the ascendancy. In Kabbalah, Lilith dwindled from an heroic self-asserter into a strangler of infants, and into the Muse of masturbation, bearing endless imps to those guilty of self-gratification. Kabbalah also married her off to Samael, the principal later Jewish name for Satan as the Angel of Death. The obsessive emphasis upon Lilith's lustfulness throughout Kabbalistic literature is an obvious indication of the large element of repression in all those Gnostic fantasies that inhabit the entire history of Kabbalah.

If Lilith is a Gnostic reversal of the *Shekhinah*, a demonic parody of the Kabbalistic pathos of attempting to exalt aspects of Exile, then it seems fair to say that the techniques of *Gematria* were a kind of parody of the sometimes sublime Kabbalistic exaltation of language, and of the arts of interpretation. For *Gematria* is interpretative freedom gone mad, in which any text can be made to mean anything. But its prevalence was itself a mark of the desperation that underlay much of Kabbalah. To open an ancient text to the experiential sufferings of contemporary men and women was the not ignoble motive of much Kabbalism. *Gematria*, with its descents into occult numerologies, is finally best viewed as an index to how tremendous the suffering was, for the pressure of the sorrow came close to destroying one of the greatest interpretative traditions in cultural history.

"Mysticism" is a word I have avoided in this essay, for Kabbalah seems to me more of an interpretative and mythical tradition than a mystical one. There were Kabbalistic ecstatics, and sub-traditions of meditative intensities, of prayer conducted in an esoteric manner. But Kabbalah differs finally from Christian or Eastern mysticism in being more a mode of intellectual speculation than a way of union with God. Like the Gnostics, the Kabbalists sought *knowledge*, but unlike the Gnostics they sought knowledge in the Book. By centering upon the Bible, Kabbalah made of itself, at its best, a critical tradition, though distinguished by more invention than critical traditions generally display. In its degeneracy, Kabbalah has sought vainly for a magical power over nature, but in its glory it sought, and found, a power of the mind over the universe of death.

*   *   *   *   *

"To see the object as in itself it really is," has been justly said to be the aim of all true criticism whatever; and in aesthetic criticism the first step towards seeing one's object as it really is, is to know one's own impression as it really is, to discriminate it, to realize it distinctly. The objects with which aesthetic criticism deals—music, poetry, artistic and accomplished forms of human life—are indeed receptacles of so many powers or forces; they possess, like the products of nature, so many virtues or qualities. What is this song or picture, this engaging personality presented in life or in a book, to me? What effect does it really produce on me? Does it give me pleasure? and if so, what sort or degree of pleasure? How is my nature modified by its presence, and under its influence? The answers to these questions are the original facts with which the aesthetic critic has to do; and, as in the study of light, of morals, of number, one must realize such primary data for oneself, or not at all. And he who experiences these impressions strongly, and drives directly at the discrimination and analysis of them, has no need to trouble himself with the abstract question what beauty is in itself, or what its exact relation to truth or experience—metaphysical questions, as unprofitable as metaphysical questions elsewhere. He may pass them all by as being, answerable or not, of no interest to him.

WALTER PATER, "Preface" to *The Renaissance* (1873)

Kabbalah and Criticism

. . . the highest grade of reality is only reached by signs . . .

—C. S. PEIRCE

Kabbalah proposes to give suffering a meaning, by way of an interpretation of Scripture that depends overtly upon an audacious figuration, the *Sefirot*. Nietzsche, in his *Genealogy of Morals*, using as his starting point the perpetual human desire to give suffering some meaning, eloquently insisted that the only meaning yet found for suffering was "the ascetic ideal." The ascetic ideal had kept mankind from nihilism, saving the will but at the expense of guilt, a guilt involving hatred of common humanity (with all natural pleasure). For the ascetic ideal is an *interpretation*, one that in turn inspires a change in the process of willing. This change signifies "a will to nothingness, a revulsion from life," yet still a purposefulness. Life thus uses ascetism in a struggle against death. Nietzsche, magnificently contrapuntal, attains a triumph in antithetical thought by declaring that to be ascetic thus is to be life-affirming. The artist in particular transforms the ascetic ideal by incarnating "the wish to be different, to be elsewhere."

Are not the *Sefirot* also, and all of Kabbalah, an incarnation of the desire for difference, and for an end to Exile? *To be different, to be elsewhere*, is a superb definition of the motive for metaphor, for the life-affirming deep motive of all poetry. Let us say (following Vico) that all religion is apotropaic litany against the dangers of nature, and so is all poetry an apotropaic litany, warding off, defending against death. From our perspective, religion is spilled poetry. Kabbalah seems to me unique among religious systems of interpretation in that it is, simply, already poetry, scarcely needing translation into the realms of the aesthetic. Beyond its direct portrayal of the mind-in-creation, Kabbalah offers both a model for the processes of poetic influence, and maps for the problematic pathways of interpretation. More audaciously than any developments in recent French criticism, Kabbalah is a theory of *writing*, but this is a theory that denies the absolute distinction between writing and inspired speech, even as it denies human distinctions between presence and absence. Kabbalah speaks of a writing before writing (Derrida's "trace"), but also of a speech before speech, a Primal Instruction preceding all traces of speech. Derrida, in the brilliance of his *Grammatology*, argues that writing is at once external and internal to speech, because writing is not an image of speech, while speech itself is already writing, since the trace it follows "must be conceived as coming before being." Derrida says that "all Occidental methods of analysis, explication, reading or interpretation" were produced "without ever posing the radical question of writing," but this is not true of Kabbalah, which is certainly an Occidental method, though an esoteric one. Kabbalah too thinks in ways not permitted by Western metaphysics, since its God is at once *Ein-Sof* and *ayin*, total presence and total absence, and all its interiors contain exteriors, while all of its effects determine its causes. But Kabbalah stops the movement of Derrida's "trace," since it has a *point* of the primordial, where presence and absence co-exist by continuous interplay. With this point, we return to the crown of the Sefirotic tree, and to the *Sefirot* as the working-model for a theory of poetic influence.

2

The Talmudists took the Scriptures as true text, and kept the line clear between text and commentary. This line wavers and breaks in the *Zohar*, which is of necessity a revisionist text. Revisionism is a reaction to the double priority and authority of both text and interpretation, Bible and the normative Judaism of rabbinic tradition. Kabbalah therefore can be viewed as a rebellion against the Jewish version of a Scene of Instruction (in the sense of that scene that I sketched in *A Map of Misreading*), which means that Kabbalah is a collective, psychic defense of the most imaginative medieval Jews against exile and persecution pressing on them *inwardly*. So, some Kabbalists spoke of a missing twenty-third letter of the Hebrew alphabet, hidden in the white spaces between the letters. From those openings the larger Torah was still to emerge, yet it was there already. This revisionist notion hoped to bring forth the invention of the Kabbalists themselves, which may recall to us that aphorism (119) of Nietzsche's *Dawn of Day*, where we are told that "all our so-called consciousness is a more or less fantastic commentary upon an unknown text, one that is perhaps unknowable but still felt."

The instrument for Kabbalistic invention began as the *Sefirot*, as we have seen. Let us return to the description of the *Sefirot*, remembering that they are at once modes-of-divination, and yet also over-determined explanations. Though there are ten *Sefirot*, only six are active in the world, and these six provide the model for the six *behinot* of Cordovero, and return as the six principles active in the fourth of the *parzufim* of Luria. *Keter, Hokmah*, and *Binah* all have to do with primordial creation, and manifest the latent potencies of God, and so have no real analogues in human creativity (a term that for the Kabbalists would have been oxymoronic, anyway). The lower seven *Sefirot*, called the *Sefirot* of "construction," are at work in creation as we know it, from the initial seven days onwards. But the last *Sefirah, Malkhut* or the *Shekhinah*, is wholly passive and receives the influence of the six "directions," the six active *Sefirot*: *Hesed, Din, Tiferet, Nezah, Hod, Yesod*. Only these six could be called poems of creation for each conceals and reveals a difference in the creative power of God, a difference that can be expressed in humanly apprehensible terms.

It must seem odd to speak of hypostases or emanative concepts as if they were poems, but the six directional *Sefirot* are precisely *like* poems or imaginative texts in the way they function. The creative insight that showed how the *Sefirot* function was provided by Moses Cordovero, the ultimate source for my own notion of "revisionary ratios," or the *behinot* as Cordovero called them. But to understand the *behinot*, we need to brood first on the kind of ideas that poems are, a brooding that for me commences with certain speculations of the major American thinker, Peirce.

All ideas, according to Peirce, divide into the three classes of Firstness, of Secondness, and of Thirdness:

Firstness is the mode of being of that which is such as it is, positively and without reference to anything else.

Secondness is the mode of being of that which is such as it is, with respect to a second but regardless of any third.

Thirdness is the mode of being of that which is such as it is, in bringing a second and third into relation to each other.

Peirce illustrates Firstness by the scarlet of royal liveries, or the hardness of anything as a possibility the *realization* of which will cause anything to be like flint. His summary is that "the unanalyzed total impression made by any manifold not thought of as actual fact, but simply as a quality as simple positive possibility of appearance is an idea of Firstness." Since I am not concerned with Peirce as philosophy, but as providing another model for interpreting poems, this summary is less useful for me than the last illustration of Firstness that he gives: "The idea of the present instant, which, whether it exists or not, is naturally thought as a point of time in which no thought can take place or any detail be separated, is an idea of Firstness."

With any idea of Secondness, Peirce says, we have the experience of effort, and the experience of resistance: "Effort only is effort by virtue of its being opposed; and no third element enters." Peirce defines "experience," in this context, as being consciousness of the action of a new feeling in destroying an old feeling. Ideas of the past are thus all ideas of Secondness, but ideas of the future are not. Every idea of the past is a dyad, a dialectic of effort and resistance, and Peirce adds his opinion "that great errors of metaphysics are due to looking at the future as something that will have been past."

When he comes to Thirdness, I confess that I do not understand what Peirce is saying, in his own terms, but find him supremely useful if I interpret him as talking about poems (which are not in his mind at all). That is, he helps me to see that poems are truly triads, ideas of Thirdness, rather than monads, as the New Critics regarded them, or dyads, as I called them in *The Anxiety of Influence*. Here is Peirce on Thirdness:

> In its genuine form, Thirdness is the triadic relation existing between a sign, its object, and the interpreting thought, itself a sign, considered as constituting the mode of being of a sign. A sign mediates between the *interpretant* sign and its object. . . . A *Third* is something which brings a First into relation to a Second . . .

Let us, by misprision, translate Peirce into the realm of poetry. A poem is an idea of Thirdness, or a triadic relation, because the sign is the new poem, its object is the precursor text (however composite, or imaginary), and the interpreting thought is the reading of the poem, but this reading is itself a sign. In the Peircean view, a poem is a mediating process between itself and a previous poem, but the mediation always belongs to the act of interpreting, which I think Peirce would have seen as being always an *evolving* act. A poem as triad is a dialectic of effort, resistance, and evolution into a future that never can become part of the past. On this account of triadic relations, there must be always an unbridgeable gap between poetry and the history of poetry, between a triad and a dyad.

Lunatic as the juxtaposition may seem, I want to contrast Peirce's vision of triads with the Neoplatonic triads of Proclus, in his *Elements of Theology*, Propositions 35–39. E. R. Dodds summarizes the triads of Proclus as: "the three moments of the Neoplatonic world-process, immanence in the cause, procession from the cause, and reversion to the cause—or identity, difference, and the overcoming of difference by identity." Iamblichus had said the monad was the cause of identity, the dyad the instigator of procession and so of difference, and the triad the origin of reversion. Dodds says of this reversion that it restored to reality the value lost in procession, but without annihilating the individuality that procession created. How? is what we want Proclus to tell us, for such a reconciliation of difference and repetition is the fundamental paradox of all originality in poetry, and would relieve the tension between poetry and the history of poetry. What Proclus tells us, ultimately, is the answer of Plotinus, that every effect at once remains *in* its cause, proceeds *from* its cause, yet also reverts *upon* its cause. Compared to the triad of Peirce, this seems to take us even further away from the kind of idea that is a poem. Translated into poetic terms, the Neoplatonic formulation would help us close the gap between poems and the history of poems, but would squeeze poems themselves into reified monads.

But poems are not so much three-fold as they are six-fold, and we will find a more adequate model if we turn from Peirce and Proclus to Cordovero, to complete our own triad of esoteric theorists. But the turning here involves a circuitous path, from Plotinus as precursor of Proclus, on through the Valentinian Gnosis that he attacked, until we reach a synthesis of Neoplatonism and Gnosticism in the Kabbalism of Cordovero, after which we will proceed to Luria again, as a more Gnosticizing Kabbalist than Cordovero.

3

"We shall insist that there is a single Intelligence that is immutable, does not swerve, and imitates its father as much as it can." Plotinus urges this insistence against the Gnostics, because Plotinus recognizes only one necessity: "that all things always exist in hierarchical dependence." It is therefore consistent that Plotinus assigns to the Gnostics, as a prime motive, the anxiety of influence:

"We hardly know what to say of the other new things they have introduced into the universe, such as their exiles, imprints, and repentances. If they mean certain affections of the soul, when she yields to repentance, or certain images of the intelligible beings themselves, they are using meaningless words *invented merely for the sake of having a sect of their own*. They imagine such fictions because they have failed to understand the ancient wisdom of the Greeks. . . . In general, their [the Gnostics'] doctrines are partly taken from Plato, while the remainder, which were invented merely to form a new system of their own, are contrary to truth. It is from Plato that they borrowed their tribunals, the rivers of Hades, and the transmigrations. They speak of several intelligible principles, Being, Intelligence, a second demiurge, and the soul. But all that comes from Plato's *Timaeus* . . .

Granted the bias of Plotinus, his thrust against the Gnosis is shrewd, for no religion ever has been so anxiety-ridden, and this anxiety was comprehensive enough to include vast and resentful anxieties-of-influence, in regard both to Plato and to the Bible. Here is a cento of passages from the Valentinian *Gospel of Truth*:

The All was searching for Him from whom it had come forth. . . . The Ignorance concerning the Father produced Anguish and Terror. And the Anguish became dense like a fog so that no one could see. Thus Error gained strength. It set to work on its own matter in the void, not knowing the Truth. It applied itself to the fashioning of a formation exerting itself to produce in beauty a substitute for Truth . . . It was a great marvel that they were in the Father without knowing Him and that it was possible for them to escape outside by their own will because they could not understand and know Him in whom they were . . . Since Deficiency came into being because they did not know the Father, therefore when they know the Father, Deficiency, at that same instant, will cease to exist. . . . Through knowledge he [the Gnostic adept] shall purge himself of diversity towards Unity, by consuming the matter within himself like a flame, darkness by light, and death by life.

Hans Jonas remarks that *the* gospel of truth, for the Valentinians, is contained in one formula, only partly embedded here, of which the full version is given only by Irenaeus, in his attack upon the Gnostics:

Perfect salvation is the cognition itself of the ineffable greatness: for since through "Ignorance" came about "Defect" and "Passion," the whole system springing from the Ignorance is dissolved by knowledge. Therefore knowledge is salvation of the inner man; and it is not corporeal, for the body is corruptible; nor is it psychical, for even the soul is a product of the defect and is as a lodging to the spirit: spiritual therefore must also be the form of salvation. Through knowledge, then, is saved the inner, spiritual man; so that to us suffices the knowledge of universal being: this is the true salvation.

What is here called "Ignorance" is parallel to the Lurianic *Zimzum* or "withdrawal"; what is here called "knowledge" is akin to the Lurianic *Tikkun* or "restitution." Aesthetically considered, as I shall soon venture, "ignorance" and "withdrawal" are modes of limitation, while "knowledge" and "restitution" are modes of representation. The triadic process of limitation, substitution, and representation, which I shall propose as the governing dialectic of Post-Enlightenment or Revisionist poetry, is what Hans Jonas calls a Gnostic concept of happening as opposed to a more orthodox or Platonic concept of being. Jonas applies it to the most famous formula of the Valentinians, which I have cited earlier:

> What makes us free is the knowledge who we were, what we have become; where we were, wherein we have been thrown; whereto we speed, wherefrom we are redeemed; what is birth and what rebirth.

Jonas observes "that the terms throughout are concepts not of being but of happening, of movement. The knowledge is of history, in which it is itself a critical event." Let us apply the same distinction between concepts to the central formula of the Valentinian Gnosis, again already cited:

> *Since* through "Ignorance" came about "Deficiency" and "Passion," *therefore* the whole system springing from the Ignorance is dissolved by Knowledge.

What this meant to the Gnostics is too complex for my purposes here, but it is important to note that the "whole system" means the cosmos. It is also crucial to observe that whereas Neoplatonism was a rather conventional theory of influence, Gnosticism was a theory of misprision, and so is a necessary model for any contemporary theory of influence as being a creative misunderstanding. Kabbalah, as a blend of Neoplatonism and Gnosticism, is as a theory of influence both a model of benign influx and a map of misprision. Zoharic Kabbalah tends towards the former, Lurianic Kabbalah towards the latter, with the Kabbalah of Cordovero a blend or balance of the two. In terms of my own theory, Cordovero provides the model for my six "revisionary ratios" with his six *behinot*, or aspects of each *Sefirah*. But Luria provides the model for my dialectic of revisionism, and the *Sefirot* themselves, the six *Sefirot* of "direction," provide the model for my six-phased Scene of Instruction. As I am pressing on in these essays towards a theory of literary history as canon-formation, I want to sketch a paradigm from the Valentinian Gnosis for my theory-in-progress, before outlining the relation of my previous formulations to Kabbalistic paradigms. I will leave for last a defense of all this esotericism, this constructing of a practical criticism out of such recondite abysses of speculation.

If we interpret the Valentinian formula cited above as a concept of happening in literary history, then we would get a statement something like this: when you *know* both precursor and ephebe, you know poetic history, but your knowing is as critical an event in that history as was the ephebe's knowing of the precursor. The remedy for literary history then is to convert its concepts from the category of being into the category of happening. To see the history of poetry as an endless, defensive civil war, indeed a family war, is to see that every idea of history relevant to the history of poetry must be a *concept of happening*. That is, when you *know* the influence relation between two poets, your knowing is a conceptualization, and your conceptualization (or misreading) is itself an event in the literary history you are writing. Indeed your *knowledge* of the later poet's misprision of his precursor is exactly as crucial a concept of happening or historical event as the poetic misprision was. Your work as an event is no more or less privileged than the later poet's event of misprision in regard to the earlier poet. Therefore the relation of the earlier to the later poet is exactly analogous to the relation of the later poet to yourself. The ephebe's misreading of the precursor is the paradigm for your misreading of the ephebe. But this is the relation of every text to every reader whatsoever. The same figurations of belatedness govern revisionary reading as govern revisionary writing. To interpret is to revise is to defend against influence. We are back at the Gnostic formulation that all reading, and all writing, constitute a kind of defensive warfare, that reading is mis-writing and writing is mis-reading. This formulation is Gnostic because for the Gnostic the unknown God is every precursor and the demiurge of misprision is every ephebe. Yet every new poet tries to see his precursor as the demiurge, and seeks to look beyond him to the unknown God, while knowing secretly that to be a strong poet is to be a demiurge.

4

I return to the *behinot* of Cordovero, after this long Gnostic digression. In his anxiety to impute no division or change to God, Cordovero elaborated a remarkable series of figurations, or "aspects" as he called them, for each *Sefirah*. As a formal intellect, rather than an intuitive one, Cordovero is unique among the masters of Kabbalah, and in some respects is almost more a theologian than a theosophist, and almost more of a philosopher of rhetoric than a theologian. Perhaps as a defense against his own Neoplatonic inclinations, Cordovero was unusually obsessed with the *Sefirot*, and particularly with their structure. For him, the *Sefirot* were at once the substance of God yet also vessels or implements quite distinct from God. To overcome this apparent contradiction, Cordovero became a highly dialectical thinker, and his ideas of emanation in particular became obsessively dialectical. Since, for literary purposes, "emanation" means "influence," we can say that Cordovero became a dialectician of influence.

It is Cordovero who notes that the process of influence begins in a dialectical alternation of images of God's presence and God's absence, in a revealing that causes concealing, and a concealing that causes revealing. Again, it is Cordovero who first sees that the *Sefirot* are concepts of happening rather than concepts of being. Each *Sefirah* is governed, according to Cordovero, by an interplay of six inner aspects or *behinot*. This interplay is what allows each *Sefirah* to emanate out from the next, but the interplay is itself dialectical, light going downward, and reflected light always glancing back.

I have suggested that, for literary purposes, each *Sefirah* can be considered as a single poem or text, meaning any poem or text. On this analogical identification, the configurations or *behinot* are precisely tropes, the figurative language that is nearly identical with all poetry. If we vary the analogical identification, and say that each *Sefirah* is a single mind or consciousness, then the *behinot* function as psychic defenses. But trope and defense are held together in the verbal image (however you want to define an image), and every intra-textual image is necessarily what I have called a "revisionary ratio," measuring the relationship between two or more texts. The sequence of Cordovero's revisionary ratios or *behinot* is one that I have found crucially instructive, for in this sequence I believe that Cordovero uncovered the normative structure of images, of tropes and psychic defenses, in many central revisionary texts, including many poems of the last three centuries. This assertion on my part is so weird, as I am aware, that I become a little anxious myself, and must assert that I myself am no Kabbalist, and hold no theosophical beliefs of any kind. I am merely a skeptic, and want only to show the shape of Cordovero's configurations, and put off until later my own surmises as to how these structural resemblances between Kabbalism and Post-Enlightenment poetry could have been produced, aside of course from the doubtless pertinent consideration that whatever misprision of both Kabbalism and poetry is involved, in this analogizing, is of course my own belated and revisionist creation, my own misreading.

The first *behinah* in any *Sefirah*, according to Cordovero, is its hidden aspect *before* it is manifested in the preceding *Sefirah*. This is to say, in literary terms, that the initial trope or image in any new poem is closely related to the *hidden presence* of the new poem in its precursor poem. I find this so suggestive and important an insight, on Cordovero's part, that I want to brood on it at some length. We are speaking here of the greatest apparent puzzle in poetic influence, which is that the deepest or most vital instances of influence are almost never phenomena of the poetic surface. Only weak poems, or the weaker elements in strong poems, immediately echo precursor poems, or directly allude to them. The fundamental phenomena of poetic influence have little to do with the borrowings of images or ideas, with sound-patterns, or with other verbal reminders of one poem by another. A poem is a deep misprision of a previous poem when we recognize the later poem as being absent rather than present on the surface of the earlier poem, and yet still being *in* the earlier poem, implicit or hidden *in* it, not yet manifest, and yet *there*. Rather than use illustrations from Cordovero here, say of the *Sefirah Din* or "stern judgment" hidden in the *Sefirah Hesed* or Covenant Love, it is better for our purposes to cite poems. Take the descendants of Shelley among the major Victorian and modern poets: Browning, Swinburne, Hardy and Yeats. There are a few passages in their earlier work that *sounded* Shelleyan, but these are irrelevant to what we are discussing. All four of these strong poets have styles almost totally antithetical to Shelley's style, yet he is the crucial precursor for all of them. When we read Browning's *Childe Roland to the Dark Tower Came*, we do not encounter in the poem any significant verbal elements that take us back to Shelley's *Ode to the West Wind*, yet it is an accurate, meaningful critical observation that the initial aspect of Browning's poem is hidden in Shelley's poem. The critical usefulness of this insight comes when we examine the opening images of Browning's poem, for these will be most meaningfully interpreted when we see them as being closely related to their poem's hidden presence in Shelley's poem. But there is also a general principle to be extracted; so many strong poems of the nineteenth and twentieth century open with dialectical images of presence and absence, with rhetorical ironies or defensive reaction-formations, because of the hiddenness of their immediate origins.

The second *behinah* of Cordovero is the actual manifestation of the particular *Sefirah* in its precursor, that is, the poem hidden in the earlier poem comes out from its concealment. But it is still *in* the earlier poem, which means that we have moved from dialectical images of presence and absence to synecdochal images of part and whole. The literary phenomenon here is a striking and frequent one, being the manifestation in a poem of a part of that poem that seems prophetic of a poem to come rather than of the poem it inhabits. A large element of what we call the contemporaneity of older poetry is involved here. Instances abound. When I was younger, Donne seemed our contemporary, because current poets kept writing verse that he had prophesied. As no one writes like that now, Donne's synecdoches seem to have receded. When critics read him now, they find him to be less of a poet whose characteristic psychic defenses involve vicissitudes of instinct, such as turning against the self, or reversal into the opposite. When W. S. Merwin or Richard Wilbur wrote in the Line of Wit, then Donne was much wittier. Now that Whitman is our contemporary again, and Donne a more archaic classic, poets like Merwin and Wilbur have moved from images of part and whole to images of fullness and emptiness. We are again in an age of metonymy.

Cordovero's third *behinah* is rather clearly a mode of metonymy, since it involves the materialization or reification of each *Sefirah* as a *Sefirah* in its own right. In literary terms, this means the precarious element in each poem that attempts the illusion of self-sufficiency and unity, or the poem as a round jar placed in slovenly Tennessee. Nothing is more unstable than this poetic element, or this aspect of a *Sefirah*. Psychically, this kind of reification is at once an undoing and an isolation, and in poems more often than not it is a regression, generally evidenced by images of a prior fullness emptying itself out. Again, Cordovero's insight exposes the *Sefirotic* emanation as a concept of happening, more a tool or vessel of power than part of the power itself.

Cordovero says that the fourth *behinah* of any *Sefirah* is the aspect that enabled its precursor to be strong enough to have emanated the later *Sefirah* outwards. This extraordinary formulation ascribes a power in the supposed cause to the supposed effect; indeed it pragmatically all but reverses cause and effect. The power of emanation, which is that of influx, becomes wholly dialectical, in this account. As a trope, Cordovero's formulation is an hyperbole, one in which higher and lower are seen as reversible categories. Psychically, the later *Sefirah* is seen as repressing its own force, in order to augment the force of its precursor, or else repressing the precursor's force, so as to augment its own. Either way, the process is uncanny, and is related to the Kabbalistic image of "channels," for which I cite Gershom Scholem, lest I be suspected of importing my own influence-obsessions into the Kabbalah.

... specific *Sefirot* stand in particular relationships of radiation with other *Sefirot* (though not necessarily with all of them). The face of one *Sefirah* turns toward another and consequently there develops between them a "channel" *(zinnor)* or influence which is not identical with actual emanation. Such channels are paths of reciprocal influence between different *Sefirot*. This process is not a one-way influx from cause to effect; it also operates from effect to cause, dialectically turning the effect into a cause.

It is useful to juxtapose Scholem's summary with Nietzsche on causalism. The error we call a "cause," Nietzsche says, is merely "a capacity to produce events that has been super-added to the events," which means that any interpretation by causality is a deception. Cordovero and Nietzsche are both talking about language, but what Nietzsche sees as a constraint put upon us, by language, is for Cordovero a supernatural gift rendered us through language.

By now it should be clear that the *behinot* are poetic images that can be regarded as the master tropes, or as the crucial mechanisms of defense. The fifth *behinah* is the *Sefirah*'s or poem's own power to emanate the *Sefirot* hidden within *it* outward, which means that as a trope the fifth *behinah* is metaphor, a dualistic image setting inside against outside. The later *Sefirot* are inside the particular *Sefirah*, yet must be radiated to outside, where they belong, by a psychic process of sublimation.

The sixth and final *behinah* is a metaleptic reversal of the fifth, for by this final aspect the following *Sefirah*, next in sequence, is emanated to its proper place, after which the whole cycle begins again with the first *behinah* of the following *Sefirah*. As a defense this is a projection, while as an image it necessarily involves an aspect of earliness succeeding one of lateness. Cordovero's theosophical cycle becomes a wheel of images, or tropes, or defenses, by which one text constantly conducts interchange with another.

5

I come now to the doctrines of Isaac Luria. Where Cordovero provided the model for the six revisionary ratios, Luria gives us the paradigm for what is even more basic in the study of poetic misprision, which is the dialectic of revisionism. The Kabbalists, like poets, pragmatically exalted rhetorical substitution, the principle of the second chance, while like poets they theoretically celebrated the first chance alone, God's creation being that first chance. Again, like poets, the Kabbalists richly confused rhetorical substitution with magic, relying upon the basic trope that God had spoken in order to form the world. The *Sefirot* are after all ten names of God, and together form the great, unutterable Name of God, which itself is a perpetually renewable act of creation. I myself find it curious that no one, in the entire history of scholarship, ever has speculated on the *literary motives* of the Kabbalists. There has been much speculation upon what has been called "a new religious impulse" (Scholem), upon charlatanry (Graetz), and upon philosophical ambitions (Ginzberg), but very little upon the palpable psychology of belatedness that Kabbalists invariably expose. Confronting, as they did, not only a closed Book, but a vast system of closed commentary, the Kabbalists refused Neo-Aristotelian philosophical reductiveness, refused normative Rabbinicism with its pious repetition, and took the Gnostic path of expansive inventiveness, though in an uneasy alliance with Jewish Neoplatonic rather than Jewish Gnostic conceptions of the Godhead. Their human anxieties, particularly after the Expulsion from Spain, were those of the endless vicissitudes of the Jewish *Galut*, the Diaspora, but their specifically *literary* anxieties centered upon a genuinely overwhelming anxiety-of-influence.

I think that this anxiety-of-influence intensified in Kabbalah with the passage from the *Zohar* to Cordovero, again from Cordovero to his pupil Luria, and after Luria with invariable reference to Luria. There is a nice juxtaposition between a remark attributed to Luria and a remark made a hundred years later by the false Messiah, Shabbetai Zevi, who had emerged from the world of Lurianic Kabbalah. Here are the two traditional remarks, which I have translated faithfully, so that only the juxtaposition is my own:

> Rabbi Isaac Luria used to say that Rabbi Moses Cordovero dealt only with the world of confusion [*olam ha-tohu*] while he, Luria, dealt with the world of restitution [*olam ha-tikkun*].
>
> Yet the learned Shabbetai Zevi used to say about Rabbi Isaac Luria that he built a fine chariot [*merkabah*] in his day but neglected to say who was riding on it.

Like Plotinus on the Valentinians, the egregious Zevi was imputing creative envy to Luria as that great sage's motive-for-metaphor. Luria's genius for the invention of new theosophical hypostases seems to me beyond comparison with anyone else in esoteric tradition. Even as Cordovero might be called the first Structuralist, I am tempted to call Luria the archetype of all Revisionists, for his dialectics-of-creation seem to me the model for all other kinds of belated creativity that came after him, from the Italian Renaissance to the present. I will not resume here the account of the Lurianic myth of creation that I gave in my preceding essay on Kabbalah, but will proceed directly to translating Luria into the terms of a revisionist poetics. After thus translating Luria, I will return to Cordovero, and to Luria's misprision of Cordovero's *behinot* as his own *parzufim* or "countenances," his own breaking-up of the *Sefirot* into their component tropes.

Kabbalah, if viewed as rhetoric, centers upon two series of tropes: first—irony, metonymy, metaphor, and then—synecdoche, hyperbole, metalepsis. I am speaking of the Lurianic or regressive Kabbalah, but a full treatment of rhetoric in the *Zohar* would uncover these same apotropaic litanies. Luria and his writing disciples, in their accounts of origins, rely upon two great composite tropes, *zimzum* and *tikkun*, and upon a connecting concept between these, *shevirat ha-kelim*, which rhetorically considered is not a trope but a violent dramatization of the process by which one verbal figure is substituted for another. *Zimzum* is initially a rhetorical irony for the act of creation, in that it means the opposite of what it appears to "say." It says "withdrawal" and means "concentration." God withdraws from a point only to concentrate Himself upon it. The image of His absence becomes one of the greatest images ever found for His presence, a presence which is intensified by the original metaphor of *mezamzem*, His holding in of His breath. If we move out of theosophy into poetry, what is the equivalent of this creative contraction? What does it mean to transform the Lurianic *zimzum* into a trope-of-limitation? What does "limitation" mean in the context of poetry?

To begin with, it means a loss-in-meaning, even an achieved dearth-of-meaning, a sense that representation cannot be achieved fully, or that representation cannot fill the void out of which the desire-for-poetry rises. Walter Pater was one of the great theorists of that void, or rather a great applier of theory to practice, the theory being for him an Hegelian modification of Plato. Hegel prophesied the death of art, the death of poetry, after our culture had run through three phases: Symbolic Art, Classical Art, Romantic Art. In the first, Form is inferior to Content; Form is under-determined, for the Idea is undeveloped or unspecified, and so imagistic representation is not wholly appropriate, for such representation must be specific. In Classical Art, Form and Content are perfectly fitted, and a determinate idea is represented by a determinate image. In Romantic Art, the relation between Form and Content breaks down, almost completely, because the Idea is no longer anterior to representation, but has so undergone internalization that its spirituality can no longer be conveyed by appropriate images.

Richard Wollheim points out that Pater's achievement was to psychologize Hegel's theory into a paradoxical vision of the role of subject-matter in art. Wollheim accurately summarizes this as the insight that "representation can exceed what it represents: and do so through representing it." I would add to Wollheim's observation only a note on Pater's sense of the experiential void, where philosophy abandons us, and art has to take over, lest we perish of the truth, a sense that Pater shared with his contemporary, Nietzsche. For the Epicurean Pater is pragmatically not far away from the theosophical Luria, when he too sees creation as rising out of the artist's withdrawal from himself, his concentration into a single point of apprehension, as here in the magnificent "Conclusion" to *The Renaissance*:

> To such a tremulous wisp constantly reforming itself on the stream, to a single sharp impression, with a sense in it, a relic more or less fleeting, of such moments gone by, what is *real* in our life fines itself down. . . .

The "real" of Walter Pater is the achieved realism of an ultimate solipsist, and circuitously that is our passage back to Luria's God, for more even than Blake's parodistic Urizen, Luria's God is the ultimate solipsist, truly and uniquely the great I Am. As a philosophical skeptic, Pater did not have the advantage of a magical theory of language, a theory that most strong poets have shared, secretly, with all Kabbalists. Pater, as Wollheim says, believed that representation could exceed what it represented and do this through the act of representing. Pater had to believe something like that, because in his own uneasy sense of belatedness he feared that Hegel might be correct in prophesying the death of art, and partly because his sense of experience so emptied experience out that art had to commence in that void, or limitation, if life itself were to go on. But though the Kabbalist poetics I am espousing is heavily influenced by Pater, who is for me (as he was for Yeats) a Sacred Book, I want to get back to Kabbalah from this particular digression.

Zimzum is a mode of limitation that rhetorically works through the series of tropes of irony, metonymy and metaphor, which means, as Kenneth Burke would say, through the processes of dialectic, reduction, and perspectivism. In psychic terms, I would add that this means we are confronting a process of imagistic limitation that arouses a series of defenses-of-limitation: reaction-formation, undoing, isolation, and regression, culminating in sublimation. *Zimzum* finally then is God's great sublimation of His own Presence, of His declaration *ehyeh asher ehyeh*, "I Will Be Present Wherever and Whenever I Will to Be Present." Sublimation thus culminates a series of *dualistic* defenses, and I think we can call limitation, in our sense, a dualizing phenomenon, for God's withdrawal necessarily creates a dualistic universe. Limitation, whether of tropes or defenses, constitutes a demand-for-language, an excessive demand, to use one of Geoffrey Hartman's formulations. In this sense, limitation recognizes a lack or defect in language that mirrors (or is mirrored by) a lack or defect in the self.

I turn then to the image of catastrophe-creation in Luria, the Shattering-of-the-Vessels that produced the world as we know it. Why translate this into poetic terms as substitution, the replacing of one image by another? The imagery of limitation centers upon absence, emptiness, and outsideness, though any poem would prefer to revel in presence, fullness, and innerness. Substitution is the actual process by which poems *work*, as images of wholeness, height and earliness work to represent desire, and restitute all inaugural limitations. The idea of substitution is faithful to the spirit of Luria because the essence of Kabbalah is to open God to the sufferings of His own creatures, and of His own creation. The vessels break so as to break, not the Godhead, but everything that is not God and yet contains His light. It is suggestive that one of the Kabbalist synonyms for the making/breaking of the vessels is "blinding," a blinding that is another inevitable emblem for the substituting patterns of figurative language in poetry.

The movement to the universe of restitution, of *tikkun*, scarcely needs translating into the poetic concept of representation. It is only a short step to go to reinforcing a potentiality for response, from the general vision of *tikkun* as redemptive restitution. The lifting up and gathering in of the sparks, the basic image of *tikkun*, can remind us that the Latin *repraesentare*, from which our word "representation" came to us by way of Old French, meant to bring something absent into presence. As a triple trope, *tikkun* poetically involves three transitions or substitutions: from irony to synecdoche, in which the absent is made present, and so is re-presented; from metonymy to hyperbole, where something emptied out is heightened again to a fullness; from metaphor to metalepsis, where something outside is placed within *inner time*, a time-yet-to-be.

Luria needed instruments for *tikkun*, and the *Sefirot* as composite tropes or Divine texts were too comprehensive for his purposes. Cordovero had taught him the *behinot*, which would have given him the range of defensive tropes or tropes of defense that could have yielded the requisite images of restitution. But Luria was too strong a poet to incur so large a guilt of indebtedness. *His* sixfold, as demonstrated in the previous essay, were the six *Sefirot* of "directions" as modified by their containment in the fourth *Parzuf, Ze'eir Anpin*, the "impatient" or "short-faced" countenance of God. Three dialectical alternations—between *Hesed* and *Din* (love and rigor), *Tiferet* and *Nezah* (beauty and endurance-unto-victory), *Hod* and *Yesod* (natural majesty and male force)—took the place of the dialectical alternations of Cordovero's *behinot*. Though I necessarily simplify these complicated theosophical models, the complications are in the first place those of a conceptual rhetoric, and need little manipulation to become models for Post-Enlightenment poems. Why this should be possible, and what is the use of this analogizing, will be my subject in the remainder of this essay.

6

Marcuse defines what the Frankfurt School of Horkheimer and Adorno had called "negative thinking" as the final form of Hegelian dialectic: "The absent must be made present because the greater part of the truth is in that which is absent." In defense of his own enterprise, his own quest for a return of the repressed, Marcuse speaks of "the effort to contradict a reality in which all logic and all speech are false to the extent that they are part of a mutilated whole." Against Marcuse, one can urge the wisdom of Kabbalah, which is the same as the insight of all belated poetry: to recover tabooed meanings does not bring about a return of the repressed. Rather, it intensifies the repression by re-activating the defensive origins of all repression.

Gnosis and Kabbalah, as I think we can now begin to see, were the first Modernisms, in our still current sense of "Modernism." A modern poem begins with a *clinamen* that depends upon the renunciation of an earlier poem. But this renunciation must be dialectical. The earlier poem (or poet) is concentrated (which means also contracted) and *made to vacate part of himself*. Since the precursor has been internalized, a crucial mental space in the ephebe is being voided. Creation begins therefore with an element in the self contracting to a primordial point. But this concentration sets up defensive reactions in the self, making the subsequent creation a catastrophe, and rendering *tikkun* or representation a hopeless quest, since there can come no reparation for an overly-defended self, and least of all *from* that self.

This creation through contraction of an internalized precursor text, which is the Kabbalistic mode, is precisely the dialectical mode of belated or Post-Enlightenment poetry. As a theory of meaning, Kabbalah tells us that meaning *is* the hurt that meaning itself is hurtful. For Kabbalah tries to restore the primal meaning that God intended when He gave Torah to Moses. But Kabbalah treats Torah as alphabet, as language itself. God gave writing, which was almost primal, except that writing was what we now would call a compulsive sublimation of a more primal Instruction. The primal *act* is that God *taught*; the primal *teaching* is *writing*. *Zimzum* is therefore in the first place Instruction. *Ein-Sof* instructs Himself by concentration, and *what* he teaches is then apparent in the *tehiru* (vacated space) as the letter *yod*. God teaches Himself His own Name, and so begins creation. Without ever saying so, the Kabbalists, like the Gnostics, have started with a belated God. And so must begin any subsequent belated creator, for every new strong poet starts with a fresh limitation that teaches him his own name, as poet, by renouncing and voiding an unbearable presence, the idea of the precursor. A turn that does not turn from anything, as posited by Derrida, is only possible for *Ein-Sof*, for only His writing is in any sense primal.

One advantage of a Kabbalistic model for a dialectic of poetic revisionism is to help us see the primacy of what I have called a Scene of Instruction in any account of poetic origins that we can offer ourselves. A maxim of sociology, at least since Erving Goffman, is the element of staging in any presentation of self in everyday life. Here is Goffman's summary of his own insight:

> . . . the performed self was seen as some kind of image, usually creditable, which the individual on stage and in character effectively attempts to induce others to hold in regard to him. While this image is entertained *concerning* the individual, so that a self is imputed to him, this self itself does not derive from its possessor, but from the

whole scene of his action, being generated by that attribute of local events which renders them interpretable by witnesses. A correctly staged and performed scene leads the audience to impute a self to a performed character, but this imputation —this self—is a *product* of a scene that comes off, and is not a *cause* of it. The self, then, as a performed character, is not an organic thing that has a specific location, whose fundamental fate is to be born, to mature, and to die; it is a dramatic effect arising diffusely from a scene that is presented, and the characteristic, the crucial concern, is whether it will be credited or discredited.

If we substitute the strong poetic self for the social self here, Goffman's insight comes even more sharply into focus, indeed experiences a version of *zimzum* or creative contraction. There is no anxiety of representation for a strong poet, as there necessarily is for Goffman's social everyman, because that anxiety was met and overcome already for the strong ephebe by the precursor (and for the Kabbalist by God). This is the particular strength that the precursor hands on, and this is why poets can be strong, not because they overcome the burdens of mimesis, but because they transcend mimesis. They confront, not the universe, but the precursors, and even if they cannot overcome the precursors, they can wrestle them to a truce.

The great lesson that Kabbalah can teach contemporary interpretation is that meaning in belated texts is always wandering meaning, even as the belated Jews were a wandering people. Meaning wanders, like human tribulation, or like error, from text to text, and within a text, from figure to figure. What governs this wandering, this errancy, is defense, the beautiful necessity of defense. For not just interpretation is defense, but meaning itself is defense, and so meaning wanders to protect itself. In its etymology, "defense" refers to "things forbidden" and to "prohibition," and we can speculate that poetic defense rises in close alliance with the notions of trespass and transgression, crucial for the self-presentation of any new strong poet.

In Hebraic tradition, all literary representation partook of transgression, unless it were canonical. But Exile is a profound stimulus to the human anxiety for literary representation. Kabbalah is a doctrine of Exile, a theory of influence made to explain Exile. Exile, in a purely literary context, wanders from the category of space to that of time, and so Exile becomes Belatedness. After the Exile from Spain, Kabbalah intensified its vision of belatedness, an intensification that culminated in the Lurianic myth in which the Creation itself became an Exile.

WORD OF THE WEEK
The Subject: God ordains certain men to hell on purpose

Isaiah 64:8 - 0 Lord, thou art our Father; we are the clay; and thou our potter; and we all are the work of thy hand.

work - Hebrew: Maaseh · an action (good or bad); product; transaction; business

Romans 9:20-23 - Who art thou that repliest against God? Shall the thing formed say to him that formed it, why hast thou made me thus? Hath not the potter the power over the clay of the same lump, to make one vessel unto honour and another unto dishonour - What if God willing to show his wrath, and to make his power known, endured with much long suffering the vessels of wrath fitted to destruction: And that he might make known the riches of his glory on the vessels of mercy, which he hath afore prepared unto glory.

fitted - Greek: katartizo · to complete thoroughly; fit; frame; arrange; prepare. Thayer says this word speaks of men whose souls God has so constituted that they cannot escape destruction; their mind is fixed that they frame destruction.

Men get angry to think that we serve a God that can do as it pleases him. They actually think that an almighty God thinks the way they think and that he could not possibly form-fit a vessel to hell merely to show his wrath and power. Paul said he does. Men have difficulty perceiving a God that predestinates men (Rom. 8:29) on whom he desires to show his grace (unmerited favor) and mercy, that he may shower them throughout eternity with the riches of his glory. We like to believe that we must give him permission if he is to operate in our hearts and minds. The Lord said, "My thoughts are not your thoughts, neither are your ways my ways. As the heavens are higher than the earth, so are my ways higher than your ways and my thoughts than your thoughts (Isaiah 55:8,9)". Our God is in the heavens: he hath done whatsoever he hath pleased (Psalms 115:3). He doeth whatsoever pleaseth him (Eccl 8:3). Thou, 0 Lord, hast done as it pleased thee (Jonah 1:14). Whatsoever the Lord pleased, that did he in heaven, and earth, and in the seas, and in all deep places (Psalms 135:6). He does all his pleasure (Isa. 46:10; Isa. 44:24-28; Eph. 1:5,9; Philippians 2:13). It is Jesus that holds the keys to death and hell (Rev. 1:18), not Satan. God will intentionally cast these evil vessels of wrath into hell and lock them up for eternity because it is not his pleasure to draw them to him (John 6:44). This doctrine angers men, though it is taught throughout the pages of God's Holy Book. Men do not have a Biblical view of the living God when they think he is not in control of all things including the minds and hearts of all men. God is not only love to the vessels of mercy, but he is a consuming fire (Deut. 4:24) upon the vessels of wrath fitted to destruction. We do not serve a God who is Superman that can only shake mountains, implode blackholes, and explode quasars. The God of the universe can harden and soften the hearts of men at will (Rom. 9:18; Ezek. 36:26). He giveth not account of any of his matters (Job 33:13).

GRACE AND TRUTH MINISTRIES
P.O. Box 1109, Hendersonville, TN 37077
Jim Brown - Bible Teacher · Local: (615) 824-8502 | Toll Free: (800) 625-5409
https://www.graceandtruth.net/

We can say then that *Zimzum*, as a composite trope of limitation, became the ultimate trope of Exile, or the ultimate psychic defense of exiled Jewry. Through *Zimzum*, God defended Himself from responsibility for unmerited evil, and for the sufferings of His people. Solomon Schecter said that the Kabbalists confronted: "an awful alternative—the dread of confusing the creature with his Creator, and the dread not less keenly felt of the *horror vacui*, or a Godless world . . . " *Zimzum*, as a radical metaphor, intervened between these alternatives, but at the price of deconstructing an over-determined tradition. This deconstruction, unlike certain contemporary ventures in that mode, was accompanied by considerable anxiety. Indeed, I am about to go against Kabbalistic tradition, by suggesting that *Zimzum* was God's anxiety. God had breathing trouble, and this trouble created the world.

I turn to Freud's lecture on "Anxiety," no. *xxv* in the *Introductory Lectures on Psychoanalysis*:

. . . We believe that in the case of the affect of anxiety we know what the early impression is which it repeats. We believe that it is in the *act of birth* that there comes about the combination of unpleasurable feelings, impulses of discharge and bodily sensations which has become the prototype of the effects of a mortal danger and has ever since been repeated by us as the state of anxiety. The immense increase of stimulation owing to the interruption of the renovation of the blood (internal respiration) was at the time the cause of the experience of anxiety; the first anxiety was thus a toxic one. The name *'Angst'*—*'angustiae,' 'Enge'* [German and Latin words for 'narrow place,' 'straits,' from same root as *'Angst'* and 'anxiety']—emphasizes the characteristic of restriction in breathing which was then present as a consequence of the real situation and is now almost invariably reinstated in the affect. . . .

Freud says that primal anxiety was toxic, and that the primal limitation was of inspiration. If the anxiety of influence be imaged as a lack of breathing space, then the voluntary limitation that allows a new poem to begin, amounts to a holding-in of the breath, until some space is cleared for it. *Zimzum*, as I've said already, derives from the verb *mezamzem*, "to draw in the breath." The Kabbalistic model here illuminates the fundamental human problem at the heart of all influence-anxiety, which is the deep, hidden identity between all psychic defense and the fear of dying.

There, for now, I must abandon the rich but troubling conceptual rhetoric of the process of *Zimzum*. The next process in the Lurianic dialectic, *Shevirath ha-kelim*, can be thought of, even in Kabbalah, as being as much a separating out and re-forming by and through differences, as a breaking-apart. It is therefore a making as well as a breaking, and has been compared by one modern scholar, Tishby, to the Aristotelian process of *catharsis*. In that sense, the *Shevirat* is a kind of cleansing, a birth of purified vessels. I have compared *Shevirat* to the process of rhetorical substitution, in which tropes of limitation and of representation alternate in replacing one another. In deconstructive terms, *Shevirat* accounts for the self-negating factor in every poem, the quest for origins that goes against the poem's own intentions. *Shevirat* accounts for the rhetoricity of poetic texts, the word-consciousness that grows more intense with time's passage.

If representation is the aesthetic translation for the Kabbalistic *tikkun*, as I have suggested, then representation is being viewed as a kind of mending process. What is being mended cannot be meaning, or presence, or form, or unity. Poems don't have any of these, and cannot be transformed into what poems have never been. You cannot, in a poem, get into the present, but poems, in repeating one another, can attain to a finer tone of repetition. But that is only an ironic vision of poetry. Poems cannot restitute, and yet they can make the gestures of restitution. They cannot reverse time, and yet they can lie against time. The Kabbalistic *tikkun* has supernatural ambitions. As Scholem says: "the *tikkun* is not so much a restoration of Creation—which though planned was never fully carried out—as its first complete fulfillment." We are not theosophists or mystics, and I do not urge another idealizing view of poetry upon us. Pragmatically, representation in belated poetry works to *remind* us of what we may never have known, yet need to believe we have known. Such reminding may be only a lesser kind of restitution, but it does strengthen the mind, almost literally it *re-minds*. Here too Kabbalah can be a powerful model for the illusory but always persuasive assertion by the mind of its own powers over all that is not mind, including language.

7

I conclude with a brief coda or apologia for the use of so esoteric and extravagant a model, in the map-making that is the interpretation of poetry. Thomas Kuhn, in his admirable book on the structure of scientific revolutions, asserts the priority of paradigms in the puzzle-solving that is normal science. According to Kuhn, anomaly leads to the emergence of new scientific theories, and Kuhn's formula for scientific progress is: from anomaly to crisis. Paradigms are prior to shared rules and assumptions, and it is when anomaly emerges, with proof that a paradigm is *contra naturam*, that discovery commences. Kuhn says that even when confronted by severe and prolonged anomalies, scientists tend not to renounce the paradigm that has led them into crisis, because no paradigm can be rejected without accepting another paradigm substituted for it. I think this is the difference between the scientist and the poet, for the precursor, however composite, cannot ever be rejected, successfully, in favor of another precursor. Further, I think that this is because a paradigm is shared by all members of a scientific community, but a precursor speaks to a single one, as Kierkegaard said, even if that precursor is as universal as John Milton was, for the two hundred years after his death. Poets have been governed, in their development, by other poets, from Homer and then Pindar to the present, and this governance always has been personal, eccentric, and even perverse.

But critics, meaning all readers, must have paradigms, and not just precursors. Western literary criticism has followed the paradigms provided by Aristotle and Plato, with the later modifications of Christian Aristotelianism and Christian Platonism, down to the recent models provided by theories as diverse as those of W. K. Wimsatt and Northrop Frye. Out of an amalgam of Nietzsche, Marx, Heidegger, Freud, and the linguists, another paradigm is now coming from France, moving upon us like that apocalyptic crimson man of Edom that Blake both celebrated and feared. In urging a Kabbalistic model, which means ultimately a Gnostic model, I am in danger of appearing to be like those Valentinian mystagogues whom Plotinus so eloquently condemned. My motives, though, are pure enough, and it may be worth remarking that I did not set out upon this enterprise with a Kabbalistic model consciously in view. But it was there nevertheless, as I groped to explain to myself why I had become obsessed with revisionary ratios, and then with tropes and defenses of limitation and of substitution. The language of Post-Enlightenment poetry, in English, betrays the patterns that were first systematized by Moses de Leon in his *Sefirot*, Moses Cordovero in his *Behinot*, and Isaac Luria in his *Parzufim*. As William Wordsworth surely never in his life had heard of Moses Cordovero, I am simply out of it, by the canons of the carrion-eaters, Old Style, of my own belated (and benighted) profession. How can the *Intimations of Immortality* Ode show a patterning of images, tropes, defenses, and ratios of revision worked out nearly three centuries before Wordsworth, by thau-maturgical rabbis of whom he had never heard? I shall venture an extravagant answer to this sensible question.

The center of my theory is that there are crucial patterns of interplay between literal and figurative meanings, in post-Miltonic poems, and these patterns, though very varied, are to a surprising degree quite definite and even over-determined. What determines them is the anxiety of influence, because it is the war against belatedness that results in certain patterns of analogous images, tropes, psychic defenses, and revisionary ratios. I do not say that these patterns produce meaning, because I do not believe that meaning is produced *in* and *by* poems, but only *between* poems. But the interaction of these patterns, between poems, suggests or opens up all possibilities of poetic meaning. The hidden roads that go from poem to poem are: limitation, substitution, representation; or the dialectic of revisionism. Even as the language of modern or post-Miltonic poetry becomes more over-determined, in a movement down to the present, so signification tends to wander, which means that a loss in meaning accompanies a tradition's temporal passage. Tropism of meaning compels tropes themselves *to be meaning*. Increasingly, a poem must be an error about poetry, and every poem begins by misreading itself. Every poetic trope is an exile from literal meaning, but the only homecoming would be the death of figuration and so the death of poetry, or the triumph of literal meaning, whatever that is. Nor is a trope a free fall, for a defensive fall is not free. The belated poet cannot substitute wholly at will, since his tropes defend against prior tropes.

Meaning, whether in modern poetry or in Kabbalah, wanders wherever anteriority threatens to take over the whole map of misreading, or the verbal universe, if that phrase be preferred. Meaning swerves, enlarges oppositely, vacates, drives down so as to rise up again, goes outside in the wan hope of getting itself more on the inside, and at last attempts to reverse anteriority by forsaking the evasions of mental space for those of mental time. A poem's images or Kabbalistic hypostases are thus types of ambivalence (not of ambiguity) that cope with the burden of anteriority. Kabbalah and modern poetry share the paradox that Kojève explored in his commentary upon Hegel's *Phenomenology*:

. . . for Hegel it is precisely in this annihilation of Being that consists the Negativity which *is* Man, that Action of Fighting and Work by which Man preserves himself in spatial Being while *destroying* it—that is, while transforming it *by the creation of hitherto unknown new things into a genuine Past*—a nonexistent and consequently nonspatial Past. . . . [my italics]

The struggle of belated poetry and of Kabbalah against anteriority could be summarized no more accurately or pungently, which may explain why Hegel, like the poets, was impressed by what he knew of Kabbalah. Time, history, freedom, and the authentic self are necessarily part of error or the swerve from origins, rather than part of the stasis of origins. For Hegel, spirit (according to Kojève) is not origin or beginning but end or result. This realization is more ambivalent in Kabbalah or in the poets, but like Hegel they know creation only as a breaking of the vessels, and they know the past only as their own creation. Hegel says that History ended in October, 1806, with Napoleon's victory at the Battle of Jena. Let us say that Poetry ended just about then also, with the Wordsworthian crisis-poem setting a pattern that subsequent strong poems seem doomed to repeat, whatever the variations of rhetorical substitution. From Wordsworth through our contemporaries, the trope defends against literal meaning in the same way that psychic defenses trope against death. Literal meaning, where belatedness is so acute in poetic consciousness, is synonymous with repetition-compulsion, and so literal meaning is thus seen as a kind of death, even as death itself seems the most literal kind of meaning.

The Talmud warns against reading Scripture by so inclined a light that the text reveals chiefly the shape of your own countenance. Kabbalah, like the poetry of the last two centuries, reads Scripture only in so inclined or figurative a defensive mode. Poets from the Renaissance through today have sought occult authority in Kabbalah, but I suspect that this seeking concealed and conceals a more professional and technical concern. However "unconsciously," poets seem to have known that the revisionary patterns of their work followed the Kabbalistic model. Not their content nor their form derived from Kabbalistic example, but rather the more crucial matter of their *stance*, their stance towards tradition and towards their precursors.

It is upon poetic stance that I come to rest here, and also upon the stance of the critic. I turn back to the Kabbalah, seeking an interpretative paradigm, for reasons akin to those that led Emerson back to Orphism and Neoplatonism. Emerson accepted the necessity of misreading, or the active figuration of the strong reader, and he accepted it with joy and confidence, as befitted the prophet of Self-Reliance. He read for the "lustres," he insisted, and he saw those lustres as emanating from His own Reason. We need to read more strenuously and more audaciously, the more we realize that we cannot escape the predicament of misreading. The Kabbalists read and interpreted with excessive audacity and extravagance; they knew that the true poem is the critic's mind, or as Emerson says, the true ship is the shipbuilder. Emerson also says: "It is remarkable that involuntarily we always read as superior beings." The Kabbalists doubtless were fearfully mistaken in their pride as interpreters, and it is true that most of their interpretations have vanished utterly. But then it is true that all but a handful of poets are fearfully mistaken in their pride also, at any time. The revisionist commits many errors in searching for an individual relation to truth, but some of those errors become the true history of strong poetry.

* * * * *

No word comes easier or oftener to the critic's pen than the word influence, *and no vaguer notion can be found among all the vague notions that compose the phantom armory of aesthetics. Yet there is nothing in the critical field that should be of greater philosophical interest or prove more rewarding to analysis than the progressive modification of one mind by the work of another.*

It often happens that the work acquires a singular value in the other mind, leading to active consequences that are impossible to foresee and in many cases will never be possible to ascertain. What we do know is that this derived activity is essential to intellectual production of all types. Whether in science or the arts, if we look for the source of an achievement we can observe that what a man does *either repeats or refutes* what someone else has done—*repeats it in other tones, refines or amplifies or simplifies it, loads or overloads it with meaning; or else rebuts, overturns, destroys and denies it, but thereby assumes it and has invisibly used it. Opposites are born from opposites.*

We say that an author is original *when we cannot trace the hidden transformations that others underwent in his mind; we mean to say that the dependence of* what he does *on* what others have done *is excessively complex and irregular. There are works in the likeness of others, and works that are the reverse of others, but there are also works of which the relation with earlier productions is so intricate that we become confused and attribute them to the direct intervention of the gods.*

(To go deeper into the subject, we should also have to discuss the influence of a mind on itself and of a work on its author. But this is not the place.)

PAUL VALÉRY, Letter about Mallarmé (1927)
(translated by Malcolm Cowley)

The Necessity of Misreading

Most of us live our lives in an uneasy alternation of two opposing superstitions: either everything that happens to us is arbitrary and haphazard or everything that happens to us is determined or even over-determined by fate, by heritage, by societal pressures, by economic factors, by systemic operations of one sort or another, or simply by our own characters and personalities. Most of us, when we read seriously, read as we live, in the same uneasy alternation between the notion that we choose what we read and the notion that it is chosen for us, by others or by tradition. We read seriously, then, pretty much as we dress or as we talk, following a range of conventions. Sometimes we may wonder at the shape of our reading, and try to decide who is setting the shape and why. That wonder is my starting point in this essay, a wonder at the shapes of literary convention, and at the phenomena of literary tradition. Who or what is the shaper of the shape? How are the phenomena of tradition formed? What is the governing dialectic, if any, that holds together the arbitrary and the over-determined in these areas?

As an academic critic, one of whose concerns is contemporary poetry, I sometimes am asked, by friends or students: "Which living, contemporary poet ought one to read?" Increasingly I've tended to answer with the names of four or five poets: Robert Penn Warren, Elizabeth Bishop, A. R. Ammons and John Ashbery in this country, Geoffrey Hill in England. However diffidently I give the answer, I am engaged in canon-formation, in trying to help decide a question that is ultimately of a sad importance: "Which poet shall live?" "They became what they beheld" is a somber formula in Blake's *Jerusalem*, akin to the popular formula: "You are what you eat." Yet we can oppose to Blake' formula a maxim of Emerson's: "What we are, that only can we see," and I suppose there could be a popular formula: "That which you are, that only can you eat," though literally of course that might seem to verge on the great taboo of cannibalism. On these models, let us compare two formulae: "You are or become what you read" and "That which you are, that only can you read." The first formula gives priority to every text over every reader; the second makes of each reader his own text. In the interplay of these two formulae, the intricacies of canon-formation work themselves out, for both formulae are true enough. Every act of reading is an exercise in belatedness, yet every such act is also defensive, and as defense it makes of interpretation a necessary misprision.

The reader is to the poem what the poet is to his precursor—every reader is therefore an ephebe, every poem a forerunner, and every reading an act of "influencing," that is, of being influenced *by* the poem and of influencing any other reader to whom your reading is communicated.

Reading is therefore misprision—or misreading—just as writing is falsification, in Oscar Wilde's sense of "lying" *[The Decay of Lying].* A *strong* reading can be defined as one that itself produces other readings—as Paul de Man says, to be productive it must insist upon its own exclusiveness and completeness, and it must deny its partialness and its necessary falsification. "Error about life is necessary for life"; error about a poem is necessary if there is to be yet another strong poem.

If tradition is, as Freud surmised, the equivalent in culture of repressed material in the mind of the individual, then rhetorically considered tradition is always an hyperbole, and the images used to describe tradition will tend to be those of height and depth. There is then something uncanny *(unheimlich)* about tradition, and tradition, used by Eliot, say, as a hedge against the daemonic, is itself, however orthodox or societal, deeply contaminated by the daemonic. The largest characteristic of tradition, on this view, is that tradition becomes an image of the heights by being driven down to the depths, or of the depths by being raised to the heights. Tradition is itself then without a referential aspect, like the Romantic Imagination or like God. Tradition is a daemonic term.

What the *Ein-Sof* or the Infinite Godhead was to the Kabbalists, or the Imagination was to the Romantic poets, tradition is now for us, the one literary sign that is not a sign, because there is no other sign to which it can refer. We cannot define tradition, therefore, and I suggest that we stop trying. But though we cannot describe what tradition is, we can describe how it works. In particular we can attempt to describe how tradition makes its choices, how it determines which poet shall live, and how and when the chosen poet is to become a classic. Rather more important, we can try to describe how the choosing and classicizing of a text itself results in the most powerful kinds of misreading.

The first principle that revisionism or historical belatedness insists upon is best stated by a double rhetorical question of Novalis: "Who has declared the Bible completed? Should the Bible not be still in the process of growth?" It is impossible not to be moved by the noble pathos of Novalis, but of course we all know, as he did, that the authority of institutional and historical Judaism and Christianity declared the Bible completed. Unlike the canon of secular literature, the Scriptures of the West are not still in the process of growth. It is instructive to consider how the Rabbis thought the Bible ended, with these words of the latecomer prophet, Malachi:

Behold, I will send you Elijah the prophet before the coming of the great and dreadful day of the LORD:
And he shall turn the heart of the fathers to the children, and the heart of the children to their fathers, lest I come and smite the earth with a curse.

The Old Testament ends with this admonishing prophecy, that the Oedipal anxieties are to be overcome, and that this will be performed by the greatest of idealized precursors, Elijah, whose ephebe will be the Messiah. The New Testament ends with a parallel prophecy, but only after a fiercely defensive insistence that the canon is indeed now closed, with these closing verses of Revelation:

For I testify unto every man that heareth the words of the prophecy of this book, If any man shall add unto these things, God shall add unto him the plagues that are written in this book:
And if any man shall take away from the words of the book of this prophecy, God shall take away his part out of the book of life, and out of the holy city, and from the things which are written in this book.
He which testifieth these things saith, Surely I come quickly: Amen. Even so, come, Lord Jesus.
The grace of our Lord Jesus Christ be with you all. Amen.

St. John the Divine declares the Bible closed, with a palpable anxiety as to how this declaration is to be enforced. The issue is *authority*, as it always is in all questions of canon-formation, and it is worth noting that both Malachi and St. John base their authority on the supposedly immediate future, on a First or a Second Coming of a reality that they seek to introject. Proleptic representation is the inevitable rhetorical resource of all canonizing discourse, which means that all canonizing must be done at the expense of the presence of the present moment. When you declare a contemporary work a permanent, classic achievement, you make it suffer an astonishing, apparent, immediate loss in meaning. Of its lateness, you have made an earliness, but only by breaking the illusion of modernity, which is the illusion that literature can be made free of literature. All canonizing of literary texts is a self-contradictory process, for by canonizing a text you are troping upon it, which means that you are misreading it. Canonization is the most extreme version of what Nietzsche called Interpretation, or the exercise of the Will-to-Power *over* texts. I am stating the thesis that canonization is the final or transumptive form of literary revisionism, and so I am compelled to re-capitulate part of what I have said about revisionary processes in my two studies of misprision, *The Anxiety of Influence* and *A Map of Misreading*, but I hope that this re-capitulation will rise above mere repetition into a finer tone.

"Influence" is an ambivalent word to use in any discourse about literature, for "Influence" is as complex a trope as language affords. "Influence" is the great *I Am* of literary discourse, and increasingly I find its aptest analogue in what the Kabbalah called the first *Sefirah*, the first attribute or name or emanative principle of God, *Keter* or the Supreme Crown. For *Keter*, like the Infinite God, is at once *ayin* or "nothingness" and *ehyeh* or I AM, absolute absence and absolute presence. The first Kabbalistic emanation is thus a dialectical entity, and rhetorically begins as a simple irony. "Influence" begins as a simple irony also, as the origins of the word indicate. "Influence" in the occult and astral sense was believed to be an invisible yet highly palpable fluid pouring onto men from the star-world, a world obviously of potencies and not of mere signs. "Influence" began then metaphysically as a wholly materialistic though occult concept, and this materialism seems to me always essential in any fresh theorizing about influence.

We all of us take it for granted that all criticism necessarily begins with an act of reading, but we are less ready to see that all poetry necessarily begins with an act of reading also. It would move us greatly if we could believe that what we call the Imagination is self-begotten. But, as even Emerson had to admit, "the originals are not original," or as Yeats's Hermit says in *Supernatural Songs*: "all must copy copies." Every idealized account of Classicism defines it as mimesis of *essential* nature, so as to fulfill and complete nature. Romanticism being antithetical or *contra naturam* had to acknowledge that nature retained priority, that nature was the *primary*. The antithetical or High Romantic thus had to achieve a super-mimesis of essential nature, it had to over-complete and over-fulfill nature, which meant that mimetic representation was not sufficient. Nature, to Romanticism, is a vast trope, and is by synecdoche a part that the so-called Imagination must complete. Over-representation demanded hyperbole and transumption, and hyperbolical and transumptive thinking moves us into areas beyond the traditional Western balancing of microcosm and macrocosm. A de-idealized vision of Classicism reveals not that nature and Homer are everywhere the same, but that mimesis of essential nature generally turns out to be the simpler act of directly imitating Homer. A de-idealized vision of Romanticism reveals that the super-mimesis of nature generally turns out to be the simpler act of imitating Milton. No one ever said that nature and Milton were everywhere the same, but also no one ever said, after Milton, that the Sublime and Milton were not everywhere the same. To *write* poetry, in the past, was to *read* Homer or Milton or Goethe or Tennyson or Pound, and to write poetry these days in the United States is to read Wallace Stevens. I take it that I am stating obvious truths. Why do we resist such truths? By "we" I mean readers, and not just readers who have turned into professional poets. There is an element in each of us that wants poetry always to be more original than it possibly can be, and I think this element is worth some speculation.

One way to understand what I mean by "influence" is to see it as a trope substituting for "tradition," a substitution that makes for a sense of loss, since "influence," unlike "tradition," is not a daemonic or a numinous term. "Tradition" invokes the Sublime, and the Grotesque; "Influence" invokes at best the picturesque, at worst the pathetic or even the bathetic. No one is ever happy about being influenced; poets can't stand it, critics are nervous about it, and all of us as students necessarily feel that we are getting or have gotten rather too much of it. To be influenced is to be taught, and while we all, at whatever age, need to go on learning, we resent more and more being taught, as we become older and crankier. Yet no one genuinely resents discovering he or she has grand precursors, at a certain saving distance. Nietzsche, increasingly wary about Schopenhauer, was delighted to discover fresh ancestors wherever he could, even in as unlikely a figure as Spinoza. "Influence," substituting for "tradition," shows us that we are nurtured by distortion, and not by apostolic succession. "Influence" exposes and de-idealizes "tradition," not by appearing as a cunning distortion of "tradition," but by showing us that all "tradition" is indistinguishable from making mistakes about anteriority. The more "tradition" is exalted, the more egregious the mistakes become. I will venture the formula that only minor or weak poets, who threaten nobody, can be read accurately. Strong poets *must* be mis-read; there are no *generous* errors to be made in apprehending them, any more than their own errors of reading are ever generous. Every strong poet caricatures tradition and every strong poet is then necessarily mis-read by the tradition that he fosters. The strongest of poets are so severely mis-read that the generally accepted, broad interpretations of their work actually tend to be the exact opposites of what the poems truly are.

Milton, who declined every dualism, is thus read wholly dualistically by the dominant modern tradition of interpretation, of which C. S. Lewis was a leading representative. Wordsworth, a wholly antithetical poet, has been read as a primary healer, a nature-thaumaturgist. Stevens, a qualified but still incessant Transcendentalist, is being read as an ironist and as an exposer of poetry's pretensions. "Influence" clearly is a very troublesome trope, and one that we substitute with continually, whether we want to or not, because "Influence" appears also to be another term for another apparent opposite, "Defense."

"Defense" is an odd notion, particularly in psychoanalysis, where it always tends to mean a rather active and aggressive process. In psychic life, as in international affairs, "defense" is frequently murderous. In the realms of the inter-poetic, defense is rather murderous also, because there defense is always *against influence*. But the inter-poetic, as I keep saying, is only a trope *for the reading-process*, and so I propose the unhappy formula that *reading is always a defensive process*, a process that I believe becomes severely quickened when we read poems. Reading is defensive warfare, however generously or joyously we read, and with whatever degree of love, for in such love or such pleasure there is more-than-usual acute ambivalence.

Before brooding on the defensive nature of reading, I want to defend my constant insistence on acknowledging tropes as being the actuality of critical discourse, even as critical argument seems to me the actual staple of poetic discourse. When current French critics talk about what they call "language," they are using "language" as a trope. Their scientism is irrelevant, and is not the issue here, but the terms of that scientism are necessarily the issue, since their value-words, including "language" and "structure," are almost wholly figurative. All of their invocations of semiology or the archeology of discourse conceal a few simple defensive tropes, and they are at least as guilty of reifying their own metaphors as any American bourgeois formalist has been. To say that the thinking subject is a fiction, and that the manipulation of language by that subject merely extends a fiction, is no more enlightening in itself than it would be to say "language" is the thinking subject, and the human psyche the object of discourse. Language is hardly in itself a privileged kind of explanation, and linguistic models are useful only for linguistic problems. The obsession with "language" is one of the clearest instances of a defensive trope in modern literary discourse, from Nietzsche to the present moment. It is a latecomer's defense, since it seeks to make of "language" a perpetual earliness, or a freshness, rather than a medium always aged by the shadows of anteriority. Shelley thought that language was the remnant of abandoned fragmented cyclic poems, and Emerson saw language as fossil poetry. Is this less persuasive than currently modish views that literature is merely a special form of language?

Shelley and Emerson, for all their visionary idealism, were not wholly out of the basic Anglo-American philosophical tradition, in which Locke is always the central figure. Even Blake, who made fun of Locke, is not from the Continental point of view a dialectical thinker, and I would suggest that the real difference between Blake and Nietzsche is the empirical strain that surprisingly persists in Blake. Dialectical thinking, whether of the various Marxist or Structuralist kinds, adapts neatly to the so-called linguistic model, just as Anglo-American empirical thinking does not, or at least not often so readily. An empirical thinker, confronted by a text, seeks a meaning. Something in him says: "If this is a complete and independent text, then it *has* a meaning." It saddens me to say that this apparently commonsensical assumption is not true. Texts don't *have* meanings, except in their relations to other texts, so that there *is* something uneasily dialectical about literary meaning. A single text has only part of a meaning; it is itself a synecdoche for a larger whole including other texts. A text is a relational event, and not a substance to be analyzed. But of course, so are we relational events or dialectical entities, rather than free-standing units. The issue is how either texts or people are to be dialectically apprehended and studied, and here Anglo-American empiricism and Continental modes can do very little to enlighten one another. Though I acknowledge from the start that poems are dialectical events, I still take up a relatively empiricist stance in regard to poems, though with a peculiar epistemo-logical twist in my empiricism. Emerson denied that there was any history; there was only biography, he said. I adapt this to saying that there is no literary history, but that while there is biography, and only biography, a truly literary biography is largely a history of the defensive misreadings of one poet by another poet. A biography becomes *literary* biography only when literary meaning is produced, and literary meaning can only result from the interpretation of literature. Poetry begins, always, when someone who is going to become a poet *reads a poem*. But I immediately add—when he *begins* to read a poem, for to see how fully he reads that poem we will have to see the poem that he himself will write *as his reading*. If we are talking about two strong poets, with a genuine difference between them, then the reading we are talking about is necessarily a mis-reading or, as I like to call it, a poetic misprision. And here I must pause to explain yet again why I insist upon mis-reading or misinterpretation as being the commonal or normal mode of poetic history.

Emerson, who disliked history enough to assert that it didn't exist, said that this human mind had invented history and so this human mind could understand and dismiss history. The Sphinx could solve its own enigma, for the Sphinx had created that enigma.

Emerson, perhaps by way of Michelet or Cousin, was following Vico, with *his* superb principle that we could only understand what we ourselves had made. A reader understanding a poem is indeed understanding his own reading of that poem. If the reading is wholly a received one, then it will not produce other readings. An entire academy can convene to declare that reading the right one, but of course it will be wrong. It will also be weak. There are weak mis-readings and strong mis-readings, just as there are weak poems and strong poems, but there are no right readings, because reading a text is necessarily the reading of a whole system of texts, and meaning is always wandering around between texts. The meaning of a poem by Stevens, say *The Snow Man* or *The Course of a Particular*, just isn't *in* the text of *The Snow Man* or *The Course of a Particular*. Nor is it in Ruskin on the Pathetic Fallacy, Shelley on the leaves and the West Wind, Emerson on the paradoxical nothingness and universalism of the Transcendent Observer, Coleridge on Dejection, Whitman on diffusing the self in air. The meaning of *The Snow Man* or *The Course of a Particular* problematically plays back and forth between its language and the language of those texts. It was in this connection that I recall venturing the apothegm that the meaning of a poem could only be another poem. Not, I point out, the *meaning* of another poem, but the other poem itself, indeed the *otherness* of the other poem.

I find it curious how many modern theorists actually talk about poems when they assert that they are talking about people. Lacan defines the

Unconscious as the discourse of the Other. That is a fine trope, though probably it is gorgeous nonsense. Freud's Unconscious is itself a powerful trope, and as a representation is painfully effective. Had Lacan said that *poetry* was the discourse of the Other, he scarcely would have been troping. If I can invoke a somewhat greater and more central man, then I question also the grand formula that Poetry is a man speaking to men. Poetry is poems speaking to a poem, and is also that poem answering back with its own defensive discourse.

With the burden of defense, I have returned to a central problem of my own stance, with its self-contradictory mixture of empirical and dialectical presuppositions. There are two defenses for self-contradiction in criticism. One would be the Emersonian-Whitmanian flamboyance of chanting that consistency is the hobgoblin of little minds, and that a large consciousness contradicts itself because it contains multitudes. Unfortunately, we have all of us arrived too late in the day to take on such flamboyance. The more appropriate defense is to look at the language of the poets, and not at any theory of language, including the poet's own, and to observe in the language of the poems a perpetual self-contradiction between empirical and dialectical assumptions. I knowingly urge critical theory to stop treating itself as a branch of philosophical discourse, and to adopt instead the pragmatic dualism of the poets themselves, as I can see not the least relationship of what we have called poetics to the actual problematics of reading poetry. A theory *of* poetry must belong *to* poetry, must *be* poetry, before it can be of any use in interpreting poems. For several hundred years now, at least, poems have located themselves smack in the midst of what Stevens called the dumbfoundering abyss between ourselves and the object, or between ourselves and other selves. The strong poets simultaneously and self-refutingly define themselves by an outrageous mixture of *two incompatible* assumptions, the first being that the poem they seek to write will stand by itself, as a unified idea of the poem, Stevens' *Anecdote of the Jar* being a defiantly parodistic example:

I placed a jar in Tennessee,
And round it was, upon a hill,
It made the slovenly wilderness
Surround that hill.

The wilderness rose up to it,
And sprawled around, no longer wild.
The jar was round upon the ground
And tall and of a port in air.

It took dominion everywhere,
The jar was gray and bare.
It did not give of bird or bush,
Like nothing else in Tennessee.

But since this *is* a strong poem, it contradicts itself, and it also asserts, with every one of its rhetorically defensive gestures, that it is only *part of a mutilated whole*, which is the fundamental gesture of the irony of all dialectic. Stevens' opening joke is purely dialectical: I placed a jar, not on a hill in Tennessee, but just *in* Tennessee, as though the whole state had reified into a single separate entity or substance. Tennessee is now a single hill and a slovenly wilderness, but because of the self-insistence of a single poetical jar Tennessee gets organized, firmed up, and so the wilderness rises up, still sprawling, but tamed.

The jar remains firmly antithetical, and everything else in Tennessee abides in the state of nature, and the whole poem starts to look like a trope of pathos, a synecdoche for desire. If we compare this little poem to our map of misreading or misprision, we will find that it follows rather faithfully the great Wordsworthian crisis-poem model, though it takes a pretty cheerful attitude towards what it insouciantly regards as a merely technical crisis, that is to say, somebody else's crisis all right, *but not mine.* The poem becomes rather like someone whistling a chorus of "The bells of hell go ting-a-ling-a-ling/ For you but not for me," but the poem remains dialectical enough to break off without going on to: "O death where is thy sting-a-ling-a-ling,/ O grave thy victory?" Stevens' anecdote isn't a triumph, it is just an anecdote, and its metaleptic conclusion introjects an antithetical future only by reminding us that all in the past is projected, and by forcing us to see that there is no present tense in the poem at all, and indeed no presence, no fullness of meaning whatsoever. The poet is a fellow who went about placing jars. If you placed the jar properly, you achieved a certain perspective. Your placing, however well you did it, was necessarily a failed metaphor, because all a metaphor does is to change a perspective, so that the phrase "a failed metaphor" becomes a tautology. A jar may be a unity, and you can do with Tennessee what you will, but as soon as you troped your jar you mutilated it, and it took dominion only by self-reduction from fullness to emptiness.

I suggest the following formula: poems are apotropaic litanies, systems of defensive tropes and troping defenses, and what they seek to ward off is essentially the abyss in their own assumptions about themselves, at once empirically reifying and dialectically ironizing. A theory of poetic influence becomes a theory of misreading because only misreading allows a poem to keep going in its own philosophical contradictions. Schizophrenia is disaster in life, and success in poetry. A strong poem starts out strong by knowing and showing that *it must be mis-read*, that it must force the reader to take up a stance that *he* knows to be untrue. The poem is a lie about itself, but it only gets to itself, by *lying against time*, and its only way of lying against time is to lie about previous poems, and it can lie about *them* only by mis-reading them, which completes our bewilderingly perverse revision of a hermeneutic circle, and returns us to the problematic question of the reader.

It is a curiosity, as I've remarked already, of much nineteenth– and twentieth-century discourse about both the nature of the human, and about ideas, that the discourse is remarkably clarified if we substitute "poem" for "person," or "poem" for "idea." The moral psychologist, philosopher or psychoanalyst is discovered to be talking about poems, and not about psyches or concepts or beliefs. Nietzsche and Freud seem to me to be major instances of this surprising displacement, but examples abound in other major speculators.

Throughout his notebook aphorisms, posthumously edited as *The Will to Power*, Nietzsche speaks of ideas as if they were poems. In the following excerpt, I have changed only one word, substituting "poem" for "ideal":

> A poem that wants to prevail or assert itself seeks to support itself (a) by a spurious origin, (b) by a pretended relationship with powerful poems already existing, (C) by the thrill of mystery, as if a power that cannot be questioned spoke through it, (d) by defamation of poems that oppose it, (e) by a mendacious doctrine of the advantages it brings with it, e.g., happiness, repose of soul, peace or the assistance of a powerful God . . .
>
> If one discovers all the defensive and protective measures by which a poem maintains itself, is it then refuted? It has employed the means by which all living things live and grow—they are one and all "immoral."

If we move from Nietzsche on an "ideal" to Nietzsche on a "thing," we still have revealing definitions of poetry, when we substitute "poem" for "thing":

> A poem is the sum of its effects, synthetically united by a concept, an image.

Nietzsche is attacking the High German metaphysical notion of the "thing-in-itself," a notion that I suspect still lingers in the Coleridgean exaltation of poetry that we have inherited. In the following excerpt, I have substituted "poem" for "thing" again:

The properties of a poem are effects on other poems:

If one removes other poems, then a poem has no properties, i.e., there is no poem without other poems, i.e., there is no poem-in-itself.

I wish now to turn the Nietzschean polemic against myself, and against the residue of metaphysics in my own ideas-of-influence, by citing another excerpt, and again substituting "poems" for "things," and "poet" for "subject." One can deny the primacy of "language" over desire, yet still acknowledge that the idea of a thinking subject, an author, writing a poem, his poem, still partakes of a fiction:

When one has grasped that the poet is not someone that creates effects, but only a fiction, much follows.

It is only after the model of the poet that we have invented the reality of poems and projected them into the medley of sensations. If we no longer believe in the effective poet, then belief also disappears in effective poems, in reciprocation, cause and effect between those phenomena that we call poems.

Influence, as I employ it, is not a doctrine of causation. It does *not* mean that an earlier poem causes a later one, that *Paradise Lost* causes *The Prelude* or *The Four Zoas*. Necessarily, therefore, influence as a composite trope for poetic tradition, indeed for poetry itself, does away not only with the idea that there are poems-in-themselves, but also with the more stubborn idea that there are poets-in-themselves. If there are no texts, then there are no authors—to be a poet is to be an inter-poet, as it were. But we must go farther yet—there are no poems, and no poets, but there is also no reader, except insofar as he or she is an interpreter. "Reading" is impossible because the received text is already a received interpretation, is already a value interpreted into a poem.

I have been citing Nietzsche, largely because he does not cease to upset me, but I have come to the point where I abandon him for Emerson, though the point is one he *seems* to share with Emerson. But this is a seeming only, and the difference between Nietzsche and Emerson here is a true difference, though it turns only upon a change in stance or attitude in regard to an agreed-upon vision. I cite another notebook passage from Nietzsche, this time with no words substituted for his:

"Interpretation," the introduction of meaning—not "explanation" (in most cases a new interpretation over an old interpretation that has become incomprehensible, that is now itself only a sign). There are no facts, everything is in flux, incomprehensible, elusive; what is relatively most enduring is our opinions.

In another of his notebook jottings, Nietzsche brooded upon self-divination or poetic God-making, speaking of himself in terms that elsewhere he applied specifically to Emerson:

So many strange things have passed before me in those timeless moments that fall into one's life as if from the moon, when one no longer has any idea how old one is or how young one will yet be.

Of Emerson, Nietzsche cunningly remarked: "He does not know how old he is already, or how young he is still going to be." Nietzsche's point about both Emerson and himself is that they both rejected belatedness, or forgot their way into a perpetual earliness. The most beautiful passage of this sort that I know of in Nietzsche is an aphorism from *Human All Too Human*, an aphorism on art as afterglow, indeed a remarkable metaleptic reversal or transumption of the Zarathustran image of the solar trajectory:

THE AFTERGLOW OF ART. Just as in old age we remember our youth and celebrate festivals of memory, so in a short time mankind will stand toward art: its relation will be that of a *touching memory* of the joys of youth. Never, perhaps, in former ages was art dealt with so seriously and thoughtfully as now when it appears to be surrounded by the magic influence of death. We call to mind that Greek city in southern Italy, which once a year still celebrates its Greek feasts, amidst tears and mourning, that foreign barbarism triumphs ever more and more over the customs its people brought with them into the land; and nowhere has Hellenism been so much appreciated, nowhere has this golden nectar been drunk with so much delight, as amongst these fast-disappearing Hellenes. The artist will soon come to be regarded as a splendid relic, and to him, as to a wonderful stranger on whose power and beauty depended the happiness of former ages, there will be paid such honor as is not often enjoyed by one of our race. The best in us is perhaps inherited from the sentiments of former times, to which it is hardly possible for us now to return by direct ways; the sun has already disappeared, but the heavens of our life are still glowing and illumined by it, although we can behold it no longer.

How does Emerson differ from this transumptive stance? Only, I think, in his insistence upon re-centering the interpretative sign, though Emerson knows also that every interpretation is doomed to dwindle down and away into incomprehensibility, indeed into another layer in a palimpsest. How then can Emerson present himself so insouciantly as a central interpreter, with a suave self-confidence that Nietzsche always envied, yet could never emulate? I verge here on the truly problematic confrontation of my own belatedness, my conscious adoption of a Kabbalistic model for interpretation. Kabbalistic models, like Emerson's Orphism or Nietzschean or Heideggerian deconstructions, exile any reader still farther away from any text. I too want to increase the distance between text and reader, to raise the rhetoricity of the reader's stance, to make the reader more self-consciously belated. How can such a reader make his misreadings more central and so stronger than any other misreader? How can there be a central misreading?

In plain terms, I am asking: What is the difference between two closely related interpretative stances, one that asks, with Nietzsche: Who is the Interpreter, and what kind of power does he seek to gain over the text? While the other says, with Emerson, that only the truth as old as oneself reaches one, that "It is God in you that responds to God without, or affirms his own words trembling on the lips of another"? How, for interpreters, do the Will to Power and Self-Reliance differ? Of course, neither interpretative stance can be rigidly defined, anyway. On the one side, there is Nietzsche's parodistic rhetoric and his bewildering perspectivism. On the other, there is Emerson's subtle antinomianism of rhetoric, and the outrageousness of his general advice: "Leave your theory, as Joseph his coat in the hand of the harlot, and flee." Still, the difference can be defined, and it is this: for Nietzsche, the trope is an error, albeit necessary and valuable; for Emerson, the trope is a defense, a life-enhancing defense. Forty years or so before Nietzsche set down his *Will to Power* thoughts upon interpretation, Emerson in 1841 filled his journal with acute insights as to why we and nature alike were tropes, and why it was the use of life to learn metonymy. Here is an Emerson *cento, circa* 1841:

> I have seen enough of the obedient sea wave forever lashing the obedient shore. I find no emblems here that speak any other language than the sleep and abandonment of my woods and blueberry pastures at home . . .
>
> The metamorphosis of Nature shows itself in nothing more than this, that there is no word in our language that cannot become typical to us of Nature by giving it emphasis. The world is a Dancer; it is a Rosary; it is a Torrent; it is a Boat; a Mist; a Spider's Snare; it is what you will; and the metaphor will hold, and it will give the imagination keen pleasure. Swifter than light the world converts itself into that thing you name, and all things find their right place under this new and capricious classification. There is nothing small or mean to the soul. It derives as grand a joy from symbolizing the Godhead or his universe under the form of a moth or a gnat as of a Lord of Hosts. Must I call the heaven and the earth a maypole and country fair with booths, or an anthill, or an old coat, in order to give you the shock of pleasure which the imagination loves and the sense of spiritual greatness? Call it a blossom, a rod, a wreath of parsley, a tamarisk-crown, a cock, a sparrow, the ear instantly hears and the spirit leaps to the trope . . .

. . . I like gardens and nurseries. Give me initiative, spermatic, prophesying, man-making words.

The underlying insight here, that the trope is a defense, is summed up in the strong essay, *Nominalist and Realist*, where both trope and defense are subsumed in the fine New England category that Emerson calls a "trick," which is a synonym that I gladly would accept for my more cumbersome "revisionary ratio." For Emerson, tropes are defensive tricks:

For Nature, who abhors mannerism, has set her heart on breaking up all styles and tricks, and it is so much easier to do what one has done before than to do a new thing, that there is a perpetual tendency to a set mode. In every conversation, even the highest, there is a certain trick, which may be soon learned by an acute person, and then that particular style continued indefinitely. Each man too is a tyrant in tendency, because he would impose his idea on others; and their trick is their natural defence. . . . If John was perfect, why are you and I alive?

In his old age, Emerson was to re-define metonymy as "seeing the same sense in things so diverse," and we can observe that the Emersonian reduction or *kenosis* which resulted in metonymy was usually the defense of isolation, or solipsism carried to an ultimate and magic realism. An isolating substitution brings about a re-centering, however unstably, whereas Nietzsche's sublimating substitution or perspectivizing metaphor necessarily de-centers. For Nietzsche, every trope is a change in perspective, in which outside becomes inside. For Emerson, every trope burns away context, and when enough context has been dissolved, a pragmatic fresh center appears. Again, for Emerson, societal and historical contexts burned away into the flux as readily as literary contexts did, and so ultimately his vision of self-reliance is one that cheerfully concedes the final reliance of the self upon the self, its condition of perfect sphericity, in which it knows and glories in its ultimate defense or trick, which is that it must be misinterpreted by every other self whatsoever.

No one would survive socially if he or she went around assuming or saying that he or she had to be misinterpreted, by everyone whosoever, but fortunately poems don't have to survive either in civil society or in a state of nature. Poems fight for survival in a state of poems, which by definition has been, is now, and is always going to be badly overpopulated. Any poem's initial problem is to make room for itself—it must force the previous poems to move over and so clear some space for it. A new poem is not unlike a small child placed with a lot of other small children in a small playroom, with a limited number of toys, and no adult supervision whatever.

I turn to that limited number of toys, whose uses are all but infinite, the tropes or turns of poetic language, for only these allow for the paradox that one poem's clearing away of another, through misprision, is manifested more by difference than by similarity. What is the difference between a reading that is criticism and a reading that is a new poem? All of us have read many critical readings, and at times we reflect or should reflect on the oddity that the criticism frequently has a stronger apparent presence than the poem upon which it comments. Indeed the criticism can seem to have more unity, more form, more meaning. Is it just that the critic has become more than adequate to the poem, or is it perhaps that the critic's illusions about the nature of poetry are governing the nature of his commentary? I will list the four largest illusions that we tend to have about the nature of a poem:

1. There is the *religious* illusion, that a poem possesses or creates a real *presence*.
2. There is the *organic* illusion, that a poem possesses or creates a kind of *unity*.
3. There is the *rhetorical* illusion, that a poem possesses or creates a definite *form*.
4. There is the *metaphysical* illusion, that a poem possesses or creates *meaning*.

The sad truth is that poems *don't have* presence, unity, form, or meaning. Presence is a faith, unity is a mistake or even a lie, form is a metaphor, and meaning is an arbitrary and now repetitious metaphysics. What then does a poem possess or create? Alas, a poem *has* nothing, and *creates* nothing. Its presence is a promise, part of the substance of things hoped for, the evidence of things not seen. Its unity is in the good will of its reader. Its form is another version of the inside/outside metaphor of the dualizing Post-Cartesian West, which means that form in poetry is always merely *a change in perspective*. Finally, its meaning is just that there is, or rather *was*, another poem. A poem is a substitution for a lost first chance, which pragmatically means for another poem. Substitution, whatever it becomes in life, is in poetry primarily a rhetorical process, which returns us to the primacy of the trope.

I don't wish to repeat here anything of what I've said already about the defensive nature of tropes, particularly in Chapter 5 of *A Map of Misreading*, where I expound the map itself. My concern now is with the history of interpretation, which means necessarily with the history of revisionism and of canon-formation in purely secular literary tradition. My suggestion is that the *history* of poetry is also governed by the primacy of the trope, and by the defensive nature of the trope. There is of course nothing particularly original about such a suggestion. Hayden White in his recent *Metahistory* has examined the governing tropes of many of the major nineteenth-century historians, and also, in an essay on Foucault, White usefully has decoded Foucault, showing Foucault's hidden reliance upon tropes in his deconstructions of the history of ideas. Similarly, Derrida and de Man have perfected the Nietzschean-Heideggerian mode of deconstruction, in which the illusion of presence in texts is cleared away, in favor of what Derrida calls the "supplementary difference," a rather baroque, ornamental name for the trope-as-misreading, which Jarry called by the Lucretian name of *clinamen*, a 'Pataphysical naming that I myself have followed. De Man has re-vivified the Nietzschean critique of history, applying it to literary modernism in particular, and subtly extending Nietzschean perspectivism so that it becomes a deconstruction of all inside/outside dichotomies that have obscured the study of Romanticism. Rather less interestingly, there have been many abortive attempts to displace literary history into the reductive categories of linguistics, or the scientism of semiotics. But literary history is itself always misprision, and so is literature always misprision, and so is criticism, as a part of literature. Like poetry, the history of poetry is necessarily apotropaic. Its prime characteristic is that it is always warding something off, always defending against real or illusory enemies, or against itself. Error is too wide a category to aid much in achieving an authentic literary history. Within the too-large vista of truth/falsehood distinctions we can locate and map the narrower and more poetic area of love/hate relationships, for psychic ambivalence is the natural context in which the reading of poetry takes place. All tropes falsify, and some falsify more than others. But it would be a hopeless quest for criticism to follow philosophy in its benighted meanderings after truth. How can it be the function of criticism to decide the truth/falsehood value of texts, when every reading of a text is itself a falsification, and when every text itself falsifies another? But, at something like this stage I always hear the protest: "What has happened to the notion of good interpretation or of accurate criticism?"

Oscar Wilde wrote many profound and beautiful essays, but his master-piece is the critical dialogue called *The Decay of Lying*. Wilde, as a good disciple of Walter Pater, was a superb antithetical critic. As his spokesman, Vivian, says in this dialogue, what is fatal to the imagination is to fall into "careless habits of accuracy." Art, fortunately, is not accurate, for it "has never once told us the truth." In a remarkable vision, Wilde's Vivian shows us Romance returning to us, by all the tropes of poetry coming to life, by all the "beautiful untrue things" crowding upon us. In the almost equally audacious dialogue, *The Critic as Artist*, Wilde denies the supposed distinction between poetry and criticism. Criticism, as the record of the critic's soul, is called by Wilde "the only civilized form of autobiography." Against Arnold, Wilde insisted that "the primary aim of the critic is to see the object as in itself it really is not." Wilde's superb denial that interpretation is a mimesis, is a good starting-point for ridding our judgments of the notion that good criticism establishes itself through sound descriptiveness. We do not speak of poems as being more or less useful, or as being right or wrong. A poem is either weak and forgettable, or else strong and so memorable. Strength here means the strength of imposition. A poet is strong because poets after him must work to evade him. A critic is strong if his readings similarly provoke other readings. What allies the strong poet and the strong critic is that there is a necessary element in their respective misreadings.

But again, I hear the question: "Why do you insist upon *misreading?*" My answer is that a reading, to be strong, must be a misreading, for no strong reading can fail to insist upon itself. A strong reading does not say: "This might mean that, or again that might mean this." There is no "this" or "that" for the strong reading. According to the strong reading, it and the text are *one*. But since the strong text is itself a strong misreading, we actually confront a doubling, in which one act of misprision displaces an earlier act of misprision. As Wilde said: "Creation is always behind the age. It is Criticism that leads us. The Critical Spirit and the World-Spirit are one."

Some of the consequences of what I am saying dismay even me. Thus, it cheers *me* up to say that the misreading of Milton's Satan by Blake and Shelley is a lot stronger than the misreading of Satan by C. S. Lewis or Charles Williams, let alone than the pitifully weak misreading of Satan by T. S. Eliot. But I am rather downcast when I reflect that the misreading of Blake and Shelley by Yeats is a lot stronger than the misreading of Blake and Shelley by Bloom. Still, I cast my vote for Oscar Wilde's insight: a strong poem lies against time, and against the strong poems before it, and a strong criticism must do the same. Nothing is gained by continuing to idealize reading, as though reading were not an art of defensive warfare. Poetic language makes of the strong reader what it will, and it chooses to make him into a liar. Interpretation is revisionism, and the strongest readers so revise as to make every text belated, and themselves as readers into children of the dawn, earlier and fresher than any completed text ever could hope to be. Every poem already written is in the evening-land. It may blaze there as the evening star, but the strong reader lurking in every one of us knows finally what Stevens knew, that no star can suffice if it remains external to us:

Likewise to say of the evening star,
The most ancient light in the most ancient sky,

That it is wholly an inner light, that it shines
From the sleepy bosom of the real, re-creates,
Searches a possible for its possibleness.

Epilogue

The Name Spoken Over the Water

At midnight he went down to the lake, to hear the name spoken over the water, but found no one there to meet him.

So he became two, one to speak the name and one to receive it.

He forgot which one was which.

Both spoke the name, and neither received it.

Then both stood to hear it, but it was not spoken.

Rabbi Isaac Luria used to say that Rabbi Moses Cordovero dealt only with the world of confusion *[olam ha-tohu]* while he, Luria, dealt with the world of restitution *[olam ha-tikkun]*.

Yet the learned Shabbetai Zevi used to say about Rabbi Isaac Luria that he built a fine chariot *[merkabah]* in his day but neglected to say who was riding on it.